MINNEAPOLIS
MURDER & MAYHEM

RON DE BEAULIEU

THE
History
PRESS

Published by The History Press
Charleston, SC
www.historypress.com

First published 2022

Manufactured in the United States

ISBN 9781467146999

Library of Congress Control Number: 2022933367

CONTENTS

CONTENTS

ACKNOWLEDGEMENTS

I wrote this book during a pandemic, and I never could have done it without the staff at the University of Minnesota–Twin Cities Libraries, who mailed books to me free of charge.

The Library of Congress's *Chronicling America* online newspaper collection was not only useful for this project but also an endless source of amusement. The archivists have done an incredible job.

The Hennepin County Library Digital Collections website provides beautiful, high-quality photos, free to download. Most of the historical photos used in this book are taken from there.

John Rodrigue, my hardworking acquisitions editor at The History Press, made me laugh with his commentary. I do not know how he keeps so many balls in the air. Senior Editor Ryan Finn helped make this book entertaining.

I was fortunate to have had many readers. Caitlin Cohn did me the favor of applying her professional editing skills to this book, making it far more readable. Carolyn Liebler, professor of sociology at the University of Minnesota, put my manuscript through the wringer, as I had hoped she would. Scarlett O'Donovan—a local character, Krav Maga instructor and true crime aficionada—provided extensive corrections on the manuscript and has also given me weekly doses of moral support. The novelist Elizabeth Sowden not only was a reader for me, but she also got me interested in this topic in the first place. My old friend Elizabeth Venditto of the Tenement Museum fact-checked me and persuaded me to cut out a less interesting chapter. The sociologist Brieanna Watters filled in some gaps in my understanding of historical cultural practices. Chen-Yu Wu endured the early rough drafts and then went out and took photos of Minneapolis for me to use in this book.

Elizabeth Dillenburg, Gail Boxrud, Gloria Deones, Rachel Fisher and Sharon Park have encouraged me throughout this process, and I am grateful to Sharon for suggesting this book project to me and getting me in touch with John Rodrigue.

Calvin and Conrad literally ran circles around me while I worked on this book. It was not helpful, but it was kind of cute.

INTRODUCTION

Minneapolis, to most outsiders, is either fly-over country or a mecca of progressive hipsterism. Locals know that the truth is darker and more intriguing. This city, and the land on which it rests, has seen revenge killings, land sharking, scalp dances, riots, murder, explosions and fires. In this book, you will find the highlights of our chaotic history.

PART I
PRE-MINNEAPOLIS

THE LAST SCALP DANCE
ON THE LAND OF MINNEAPOLIS

On May 27, 1825, a few hundred Ojibwes canoed down the Mississippi River and camped on the east bank, across from Fort Snelling. ("Ojibwe," also "Ojibwa," is a modern spelling of "Chippewa.") Before crossing the river, they set up their tents. They planned to stay for a little while to visit the Indian agency near the fort.

Within hours, Dakota warriors arrived in canoes.[1] They alighted on the riverbank and attacked the Ojibwes. The Dakota warriors scalped women and children, crossed the river to the west bank and ran toward the prairie that is now Minneapolis. There they danced around the scalps. This was not the last scalp dance on that land.

It wasn't the first either. The initial salvo in the Ojibwe-Dakota conflict is lost to memory, as is the case long-standing international feuds the world over. Whichever side it was that committed the original offense against its enemy centuries ago hardly matters nowadays. It was the same with the historic rivalry between these two nations in Minnesota.[2] The Dakota Sioux filled most of Minnesota, leading early European explorers to call the region "Suland" (Sioux Land). The Ojibwes lived all around Lake Superior to the northeast. Other nations, including the Winnebago and the Sac and Fox, lived in or near the region as well, but they were not a party to the specific feud between the Dakotas and Ojibwes.

European entanglements farther east intensified the conflict. The English armed the already-powerful Iroquois and enabled them to drive out rivals. Their early adoption of the combination of Native battle tactics with European firearms made them nearly invincible.

The Ojibwes were already migrating west, in fulfillment of an ancient prophecy, but the Iroquois and their allies shoved them out faster than they had planned. In the land that would become the state of Minnesota, the Ojibwes faced intense competition for hunting grounds with Dakotas. The encouragement from European traders to hunt fauna to extinction for their furs only made matters worse. It was not greed for traders' goods that motivated the Natives to do this. Firearms were among the most prized items that Natives received from the traders in exchange for pelts. The traders' weapons gave rivals an extreme advantage. This led to an unending drive to outdo each other's fur acquisitions so as to secure more arms. By the 1830s, the situation was heading toward existential threat for those who could not compete.

White settlers were moving farther and farther west as well, tying up land that had before been used for hunting, in order to plant crops and let their livestock graze. Before, the Dakotas had circulated among different but established settlements as soon as the game animal population began to thin out. This change of home would allow for animal repopulation, so that there was never real scarcity. All of that was changing with new pressures.

Rivalries among Native groups had typically manifested in fly-by-night raids, not drawn-out battles. In modern terms, all sides involved engaged exclusively in guerrilla warfare. Raids had once occurred occasionally, but now that there was so much more at stake, they went down at nearly every opportunity. They would sometimes kill their enemies on sight. Then, the victim's community would retaliate, sparking further retaliation, such that a single killing could snowball into a years-long cycle of eye-for-an-eye homicide.

The Dakota-Ojibwe feud was by no means the origin of retributive justice in North America. It's a common system of law, found in cultures all over the world. Pre-Christian Scandinavia had formal courts and judges who ruled on, and oversaw, the fair practice of retributive justice. In England, where it was called "blood feud," William of Normandy tried and failed to stamp it out in the north of the country. It is widely believed that the infamous family grudges among white communities in Appalachia are a legacy of Scotland's version of it. North America would have been exceptional if retributive justice *hadn't* organically developed here. But there was no denying that it was worse now.

***

Man of the Sky[3] was born in the mid-1880s to a Dakota mother and French father. He lived a typical Dakota life, but his son-in-law, the Indian agent for the Dakotas, tried to persuade him to settle down and take up European-style agriculture. With population pressure from the East in the form of both Ojibwes and whites, there was something to be said for staking out a permanent settlement that couldn't be pulled out from under the Dakotas in their absence, which was currently a risk if they traveled to other hunting grounds. With European agriculture, said the agent, they could cultivate and tend designated fields that wouldn't be taken from them.

Despite his fondness for the agent, Man of the Sky didn't take his advice. A few Dakota chiefs[4] were interested, but that interest did not extend to implementation. Man of the Sky changed his mind in the late winter of 1828. He was with a hunting party on the plains when he and his fellows were caught in a snowstorm. They survived, but barely, after three days of being buried in snow, with only their blankets for shelter and with slim rations. The time had come, Man of the Sky decided, to take his son-in-law's recommendation and settle down with what the agent had told him would be a steady, stable food supply.

The agent thought that the shore of Bde Maka Ska—in what is now Lakewood Cemetery—would be a good location for his father-in-law's project. He furnished Man of the Sky with agricultural equipment that he paid for out of his own pocket. Around the same time, a pair of wannabe missionaries, two fresh-faced, highly unqualified white brothers in their early twenties, Samuel and Gideon Pond, turned up on his doorstep to volunteer their services to the Dakotas. The agent sent them along to Bde Maka Ska. Man of the Sky brought residents. He went to the village of Black Dog, who had told Man of the Sky that he himself would have tried his hand at white-style agriculture if he had been a younger man. There, Man of the Sky recruited families who felt the same way as the elderly Black Dog. The year after his daughter, The Day Sets Taliaferro, gave birth to his granddaughter, Mary, Man of the Sky was elected chief of the experimental Dakota agricultural village. Ten years later, the fallout from a cycle of raids between the Dakotas and Ojibwes would end the experiment.

MARY'S FATHER, LAWRENCE TALIAFERRO, was born into an old Virginia family. His distant immigrant ancestors had Anglicized the pronunciation, though not the spelling, of their name to "Tolliver." They were a wealthy slaveholding family who owned the Whitehall Plantation, where Lawrence was born in 1794. Lawrence was exactly the sort of person whom a lavish, privileged upbringing would be expected to produce. He was a perpetually petulant, self-absorbed, spoiled brat, to the immense irritation of his detractors and the amusement of his friends. The ever-flowing income from the forced labor of others made him generous. He was arrogant but trustworthy and believed himself to be a very good man. He had first served in the U.S. Army during the War of 1812, when he was eighteen years old, and he was now a major. In 1820, he was appointed Indian agent for the Dakotas.

Taliaferro must have known, on some level, that it is wrong to hold other people in captivity and force them to work for you, because he planned to free them at some future date. For this reason, he never sold them. There was only one exception to his no-sell rule. As justice of the peace, Taliaferro officiated the wedding of Harriet Robinson, whom he "owned," to Dred Scott in 1836. Taliaferro then sold Mrs. Scott to Dr. John Emerson, the Fort Snelling military surgeon and "owner" of Dred Scott, so that the couple would stay together. One could argue that Taliaferro also could have kept them together if he had bought Mr. Scott's freedom and freed Mrs. Scott so that the spouses could do as they pleased, and one would be right. Eventually, he would release every single enslaved person in his household, although why he took so long in doing it is unclear.

Taliaferro had custody of Mary, the only child he would ever have, even after a second marriage to a white woman back east. He extended the affection he felt for Mary to all of her mother's kin, with the downside that this affection was paternal. He genuinely felt that all the Dakotas were his children—and yes, he did call them that. No one can dispute that the Dakotas needed allies. Along with other North American nations, the Dakotas had been greatly reduced in power and numbers by this time. The traders had introduced smallpox, venereal disease, influenza and measles to their populations, which had had no prior exposure. It is estimated that these diseases wiped out 90 percent of North Americans. It is indicative of how shriveled the hunting grounds had become in terms of acreage, and how many game animals had been killed for traders' pelts, that the Dakotas and Ojibwes now struggled to find enough food to go around.

Fur traders resented Taliaferro's efforts to prevent them from taking advantage of the Dakotas. Before his arrival at the fort, and behind his back, the traders persuaded the Dakotas with whom they did business to sign deeds and contracts written in untranslated English and got them heavily drunk so that they couldn't think straight when they did so. The Dakotas had no way of knowing the market value of the goods they either bought or sold. The traders underpaid them and overcharged them, miring them in debt.

Taliaferro was also unpopular with some of the Dakotas because he was so patronizing. It frustrated them that he inserted himself into their dealings with the traders. He also tried to prevent the Dakotas from partying with their drinking buddies, the enlisted men, whom he believed to be a bad influence on his "children."

Taliaferro and Colonel Josiah Snelling, the commandant who oversaw the fort's construction, immediately got to work in 1820, organizing peace talks between Ojibwe and Dakota chiefs. Many of them already wanted peace. The chiefs would show up, cooperate and reach an agreement, and then their men would resume fighting, sometimes within twenty-four hours. Having done this without success for five years, Taliaferro sought a more official approach. In preparation for the August 19, 1825 Multinational Treaty at Prairie du Chien, Taliaferro arranged for a surveyed map of the area, with a firm, on-paper boundary between Ojibwe and Dakota territory for living and hunting.[5] Taliaferro made sure that the treaty specified the boundary line. One of the provisions was that the Dakotas and Ojibwes would stay on their own sides and leave each other alone. The leaders signed it, pledging to respect the line that had been "drawn and marked by the white man's science."[6]

Taliaferro and his fellow American officials (at that time, Natives did not self-identify as "Americans," and they reserved that term for the people of the United States) may have been temporarily satisfied, but the Native signatories "concurred in the arrangement...proposed by the U.S. Commissioners... [only because they thought] that compulsion would otherwise be used. But they were not satisfied, nor had they reason to be, for their ancient limits were grievously abridged."[7] A tragedy befell the Natives at the Prairie du Chien council that further undermined the treaty. Their U.S. hosts provided them with food, and many of the Natives came down with dysentery. Some of them died on the spot, and many others died on the way home. The survivors could not help but wonder if they had been poisoned. They had had little reason to trust the Americans or their intentions before that, and now they had even less. They acted accordingly. "The [Natives] paid little respect to [Taliaferro's] air line, but went on with their accustomed raids."[8]

TWELVE YEARS LATER, IN 1837, Taliaferro traveled with some Dakota chiefs to Washington, D.C., to negotiate a treaty with the federal government. He was very proud of this effort and advocated strongly for Dakota interests. While Man of the Sky may have appreciated his son-in-law's advocacy, he was beginning to have his doubts about taking advice from him. On October 5 of that same year, Man of the Sky attended a council between the local Dakotas and some visiting Sac and Fox bands. There, he expressed frustration with Taliaferro, on whose advice he and his village had refrained from executing retributive justice against rival nations who had raided and killed members of his community:

> *My ears are always open to good counsel, but I think* [that you] *should take a stick and bore the ears of* [our enemies[9]]. *They appear to shut their ears when they come into council. I always thought myself and my people would be made happy by listening to your advice. But I begin to think the more we listen, the more we are imposed upon by other tribes. Had I been foolish and given foolish course to my young men, you would not have seen me here today. I might have been at home doing mischief, seeking to revenge what these people have provoked. I have been struck by these men eight times and have lost many of my people.*[10]

And yet, his village kept growing. Food was increasingly scarce among the nearby villages, and Man of the Sky shared with them what his own people had harvested. Taliaferro counseled him against this, telling him that generosity was contrary to his own village's self-interest. Man of the Sky ignored him. He knew that his neighbors would have extended the same courtesy to his village. Besides, the chief was probably beginning to doubt Taliaferro's advice on all fronts. Man of the Sky's seemingly boundless patience would soon snap. Six months after Man of the Sky told Taliaferro how he really felt at the October council, he would reach his breaking point.

IN APRIL 1838, THIRTY-SEVEN-YEAR-OLD Hole in the Day,[11] an Ojibwe chief from Gull River, was on an excursion with nine companions. They were hunting in modern-day Swift County in central Minnesota, and encountered a group of Dakotas, mostly women and children. Hole in the Day and his friends pretended to mean them no harm, and the Dakotas treated them with hospitality, offering them delicacies with their meal. Come nightfall, the

Ojibwe party shot eleven Dakotas, several of whom were Man of the Sky's in-laws. They also wounded one child and kidnapped another.

On July 16, Man of the Sky told Taliaferro that the massacre had cost him dearly. Not only had Hole in the Day taken his family members, but he was also reducing the land on which Dakotas could safely hunt—and they were hungry. The great agricultural experiment was about to fail, said Man of the Sky, because they were going to have to kill their cattle to make up for the loss of game. One month later, Taliaferro got word that they had gone through with it. He sent more cattle to them to make up for it.

More cattle did not soften the village's rage. Man of the Sky had been married to Chasapawin for about three decades, and he was close with her family. The losses that he suffered in April tipped him over the edge. His brother-in-law, Red Bird, shared his grief. Red Bird was the Bde Maka Ska medicine man. As far as white observers could tell, it was medicine men, not chiefs, who held power within the community. Villages elected chiefs to represent them, and they were generally given the final word in how the community would proceed. But medicine men were given far more authority over day-to-day matters. In modern terms (if the Euro-American impression was correct), chiefs were heads of state, while medicine men were heads of government. They were far more than healers or religious leaders, although they were those things too. Red Bird and Man of the Sky nursed each other's anger, and war dances filled their days.

Taliaferro sent a message to the Ojibwes to keep their distance from Fort Snelling, "as the [Dakotas] ha[d] sworn vengeance if [Hole in the Day] [came] under the walls or the gate of the fort."[12] Hole in the Day, a deeply contrary man, came with a group of friends to the Falls of St. Anthony on Thursday, August 2. In his party were a fellow Ojibwe, White Fisher, two Ottawa men and a woman. Ottawas are so closely associated with Ojibwes[13] that they have long had some joint communities, and the Grand Traverse Band of Ottawa and Chippewa Indians lives to this day as a single nation on Michigan's Lower Peninsula.

The day after the Ojibwe and Ottawa travelers arrived, Taliaferro went to his father-in-law's village on routine official business. He was there until the evening, when Samuel Pond came to him. Pond told him that a party of armed Dakotas was on the way to Coldwater Spring, where they planned to kill Hole in the Day. Taliaferro tore off in his carriage. He drove seven and a half miles at top speed.

COLDWATER SPRING, IN THE Mississippi National River and Recreation Area, is Hennepin County's sole remaining major natural spring. It is a sacred site for the Dakotas and had supplied the water for Coldspring's Well in Camp Coldwater, which had temporarily housed soldiers in the early 1820s during the construction of Fort Snelling. Three young Dakota brothers, whose relatives had been killed in the raid in April, anticipated that Hole in the Day's party would visit Mrs. Patrick Quinn, an Ojibwe woman who lived near the spring. The Dakota brothers hid close to her home and waited.

As the first shot range out, Taliaferro arrived. He leaped from his carriage to the chorus of four or five more shots. An Ottawa man dressed in Hole in the Day's usual outfit took a bullet and fell. He died immediately. The other Ottawa man was injured. One of the Dakota brothers grabbed the wounded Ottawa and began to scalp him. White Fisher shot the scalper, stopping him in his tracks but not killing him. Taliaferro knew the brothers' father, Toh Kah. He knew that he could find them again. He had Hole in the Day and all of his friends, dead and alive, brought to the fort a mile away. At nine

Coldspring's Well (Camp Coldwater), between Fort Snelling and Minnehaha Falls. *Hennepin County Library Digital Collections.*

Environs of Coldspring's Well. *Hennepin County Library Digital Collections.*

The area near Coldwater Spring today, perhaps not far from the site of the ambush. *Author's collection.*

Round tower at Fort Snelling. This may have been used as a guardhouse at that time. *Author's collection.*

o'clock that evening, he sent another Dakota man to the Fort Snelling guard house as a hostage, to discourage further violence.

In the morning, Taliaferro met with Major Plympton. They decided to summon the local chiefs and demand that they hand over the shooters. Returning to the agency, Taliaferro found that some of the chiefs were already there, including his father-in-law. They were waiting for him. They all sat down in the agency's vast council hall, in which hung a U.S. flag. Scattered around the flag were British war memorabilia that the Dakotas had received for service to the British army during the War of 1812. Man of the Sky may have fought with the force that took over Fort Mackinac from the United States, as well as in the battle to recapture Prairie du Chien from the U.S. Army in 1814. He had proudly displayed his medals from the British until the 1820s, when Taliaferro and Colonel Snelling began to offer exchanges of British medals for U.S. ones as a show of good will.

Taliaferro was the first to speak: "My friends[,] we have determined to send for you—but we are pleased to see you come forward without a message. I expect you to do whatever your brother, [Maj. Plympton] may desire." Taliaferro further explained that the issue was not the attack itself, but that they had committed it at Cold Spring, so close to the fortress. He then sat back to take notes.[14]

Plympton expressed his pleasure at seeing their guests willing to talk so soon, addressing them as "friends," the same as Taliaferro had done. Plympton added, "I notice many old & familiar faces—, and grey heads that time has render[ed] furrow[ed] & grey like my own." Then, he took off the gloves. "I wish to know if you after so many years of peace—wish to break with us—if so I desire to know it." It was quite a leap to assume that because a few young men hadn't considered the implications of choice of location for where they attempted to assassinate their relative's killer, all of the Dakota villages were ready for war.

Plympton wasn't done escalating. "It is my trade to fight—& our soldiers are ready I repeat that if you are disposed to have difficulty with us say, or by delivering up those who have done mischief show us that you desire peace." He went on to discuss his favorite hobby: exercising authority. "I hold a check upon my soldiers in the Fort & I expect you the chief to hold your own people in check." He proceeded to pay Taliaferro a backhanded compliment, insinuating that he was too generous to the Dakotas because he wanted to be friends with them so badly.

The Good Road, an impetuous young chief from a village by Man of the Sky's, spoke up. "My Brother[,] the words which you use today I did not hear from [Taliaferro]…but I do not feel this day disposed to loose [sic] the friendship of the whites." He explained that he had come to the fort the day before, not knowing that Taliaferro would be away at Man of the Sky's village. Plympton had been unavailable, too. The Good Road had come to warn them that Hole in the Day and his party should stay within the walls of the fortress, knowing that the Dakotas wanted revenge against them. He asserted again that he and the other Dakota chiefs only wanted peace with the whites. He concluded hotly, "I pass over one word (war) which you have <u>used</u> in your remarks to us."[15]

Plympton replied that if the Dakota chiefs were to make peace with Hole in the Day, then he would only incarcerate the assailants. This was a veiled threat. If they did not do this, then he would consider *all* of them enemies.

Koc Mo Ko, chief of a village neighboring Man of the Sky and The Good Road's, issued a non-apology for the ages: "I am sorry that the Hole in the Day came down here so soon after the murder of 13 of our people. I felt mortified, and vexed that he should have come here."

Mah zah Hoh ta, a chief from a village further away, expressed shame at the actions of the Dakota ambushers, but added bitterly, "Hole in the Day… [h]as no more sense than a dog to do as he has done, and then come down here." Mah zah Hoh ta explained that in April "he murdered our people in cold blood—their relatives were here & more lately my uncle was killed [by Ojibwe warriors] at Lake Pepin. It hurts our feelings all these things[.]" Besides, it balanced out: the death of one Ottawa and the injury of another at Cold Spring was the equivalent of the brother's loss of a relative at Lake Pepin and the injury of the third brother at Cold Spring. Yet, said Mah zah Hoh ta, "you still make a demand for the [two unharmed brothers]." According to their custom, the matter was already settled. There was no need to further sanction the Dakota ambushers. Koc Mo Ko grudgingly mused, "I suppose I must comply with your request—but what is to be done with the Hole in the Day for his <u>acts</u>[?]" Although no one mentioned it at the council, Hole in the Day had almost certainly expected trouble. Why else would he have swapped clothes with his friend, who ended up taking the bullet that was meant for him?

Skush Kah nah was the most bitter, and he had good cause for bitterness. He had lost nephews and nieces to Ojibwe slaughter, and Hole in the Day had been responsible for it. Skush Kah nah had come across him at one point over the previous two days and had to turn away. If he had so much as looked at him longer, he would have done him violence. He joined the others in saying that the Cold Spring casualties satisfied the retributive justice system under which they operated.

The elderly chief Grand Soldier did not trust himself to be tactful, and he said as much. He informed Plympton that he and the other chiefs would discuss it among themselves and then tell Plympton whether or not they would do as he asked. "It is unnecessary to talk much[,]" said Plympton. "I have demanded the accused and they must be brought." By that word, *accused*, Plympton made it clear that he saw the young men as criminals.

Toh Kah's sons lived at Red Wing about fifty miles southeast, but they were currently staying at Mud Lake, in modern-day West St. Paul. Taliaferro instructed his father-in-law and his neighbors to bring them to the Indian agency. Within thirty minutes, the chiefs left, returning at about 5:30 p.m.

They brought the young brothers to the Indian agency. Their mother accompanied them. She assumed that Plympton would have them shot, and she begged Taliaferro to advocate for them. She had borne seven sons and lost four of them already. A fifth one, the boy who had been shot by White Fisher, was dying from his wound. Taliaferro wrote later in his journal that day, "[I]f these two [brothers] now put in my hands were <u>shot</u>—Her all was gone. <u>Can any one imagine my situation</u>?"[16] Still, he brought the brothers to the fort, telling the chiefs to come as well. As they went, the brothers sang a traditional death song, having made the same assumption as their mother. They were left in the guardhouse for the night. Taliaferro sent for the chiefs of the Red Wing village.

The next day was Sunday. If Taliaferro had hoped to rest on the Sabbath, then he was disappointed. The Ottawa man who had been shot while wearing Hole in the Day's clothes had been buried on the Fort Snelling reservation. Taliaferro had to convene another council, as there had been an attempt overnight to dig up the body. He and Plympton united in a demand that the men who had tried their hand at grave-robbing be turned over to Plympton. It does not appear that they were ever identified.

On Monday the fifth, Taliaferro learned that prior to the ambush, some U.S. soldiers, Canadian traders and mixed-race people living among the white civilians had been taunting the local Dakota for not avenging their fellows' deaths. Taliaferro blamed these instigators for the brothers' actions, looking for any excuse to deflect blame from his "children." He either did not know, or had chosen to forget, that his own mixed-race father-in-law had been leading war dances in preparation for retaliation for the killings in April. While Taliaferro could not send soldiers away from the fort or Canadian traders away from their trading post, he did wish that he could kick out the mixed-race instigators before they could provoke another incident.

That evening, Plympton sent Hole in the Day and friends across the river, toward home. Only the wounded member of his party remained in the hospital at the fort.

Finally, on Tuesday, August 7, the Red Wing chiefs Wacouta and Iron Cloud came to the agency with local Dakota chiefs. When they arrived at 11:30 a.m., they asked to see Plympton. Iron Cloud begged Plympton to reunite him with the brothers: "They are a part of my body and if you are willing you may…place me along side of them." He accepted that the brothers had done wrong but argued that "they did not know the consequence of their act." If he had been frank, then he would have said that many other men besides Toh Kah's sons would not have been able to predict the consequences, either. "I hope you will take pitty [*sic*] upon me before the <u>sun</u> goes down let me have my friends be returned."

Plympton replied with a non-sequitur: "Your people have…gone on to kill our cattle—horses & hogs to a large amount—also insulted my men by cocking their guns & firing arrows at them—by pulling down my fences & grave yard." This wasn't *just* about the recent ambush. It was about Plympton's accumulated grievances against the Dakotas. "[L]astly [your people] commit[ted] murder on this sacred ground by killing the chippewas under the guns of the Fort." Having concluded his rant with that bit of puffery, Plympton told Wacouta and Iron Cloud that he would let the young men go free, if the two chiefs would apply their own sanctions to Plympton's satisfaction. He let them think about it overnight.

Wednesday morning found Taliaferro in a state. He had attempted to further investigate the instigators of the ambush. His inquiry into bad actors among the traders had kicked off a game of telephone that resulted in Plympton getting complaints against the Indian agent himself, embellished in his disfavor. Plympton took the complaints at face value and sent an officious, offensive note to Taliaferro. Taliaferro issued an official reply to say that the traders had put words in his mouth. Taliaferro was enraged. He had been an Indian agent for eighteen years, and everyone knew that he was a forthright man who had never done anything to incur such censure.

On the advice of the traders, Plympton ordered Taliaferro to abandon his inquiry. Taliaferro, who had been a soldier for twenty-six years, was contemplating disobedience. "I feel myself too strongly fortified under a conscientious rectitude of action & purpose—to listen to orders effected [*sic*] by the idle gab of a sett [*sic*] of ignorant <u>Asses</u>." He didn't respect Plympton's sources or judgment or orders.

At two o'clock that afternoon, Taliaferro was back in the council hall, attending the council with Plympton and the Dakota chiefs. Taliaferro told the chiefs that Plympton was ready for their decision on whether or not Wacouta and Iron Cloud should punish Toh Kah's sons.

Iron Cloud replied at length. In sum, he said that the ambushers were a couple of "foolish men" who didn't realize that they were doing wrong. He expressed his hope that his "friend," meaning Plympton, would safely return the brothers to him.

Plympton told him irritably, "I called to learn what decision the chiefs had come to on my proposition of yesterday—there is no use for long speeches—come at [once to] the point." Plympton's impatience with speechifying rendered him uniquely ill-suited for diplomacy, but he wasn't there to keep the peace. He was there to flex the army's muscles. The point was: "Will you punish these men if I bring them out of the Fort to this Agency[?] I want a straight forward answer."

Big Thunder of Kaposia, a village in the general area of what is now St. Paul, uttered some polite nothings, and Wacouta finally acquiesced to Plympton's demands. The Good Road, recalling a statement that Plympton had made earlier (and which Taliaferro had not recorded at the time), interjected, "My fr[i]end[,]" meaning Plympton, "you [said] if you had sent out 200 of your troops when this thing [took] place they might have done us great damage." He met Plympton's bullying with bluster. "What do you suppose that we should have been about at that time?"

At these councils, the men addressed each other and the translator would facilitate communication. Plympton shed any remaining pretense of respect. Instead of speaking directly to The Good Road, he turned to the translator, Colin Campbell. "Tell the Good Road," said Plympton, "[that] I am not boasting nor have I boasted—therefore I shall not hear him do so." The other Dakota chiefs fell over themselves to shut down The Good Road and to express their agreement with Plympton. They had had their fill of hotheaded young men dragging them into conflict with the commandant.

Plympton then implied that Iron Cloud was weak if he did not agree to do as Plympton demanded. Iron Cloud caved. "I am [strong enough], & if you will bring them out I will…satisfy you I can do as I say." Iron Cloud must have realized that he had no choice. The price of the youths' freedom was Plympton's satisfaction.

The brothers were brought from the guardhouse, back to the Indian Agency. There were some Dakota women present who wept. The ceremony that awaited the brothers bore some similarity to the ritualistic cutting-off of an offenders' uniform that characterized the traditional "cashiering" of European military men upon dishonorable discharge, a practice currently enacted on modern-day disgraced U.S. law enforcement and corrections officers. Wacouta and Iron Cloud's Red Wing warriors cut up the brothers' clothing from the outside in, cropped their hair and beat them with sticks.

Taliaferro was satisfied nearly to the point of cheerfulness. *Everyone* was satisfied, he thought. The Dakotas were satisfied that the boys were returned to their family unharmed. The Ojibwes were satisfied that they had caused an equal number of casualties to Toh Kah's family as they had experienced themselves. Taliaferro was delighted to receive the news that the trader whom he held primarily responsible for instigation had gotten into hot water.

It was over. "This unfortunate affair was thus amicably settled," Taliaferro told himself.[17]

Almost a year after the ambush, in mid-June 1839, nine hundred Ojibwes and 1,200 Dakotas converged on Taliaferro's agency. The Dakotas had come for the annuities and rations that were due to them by the Dakota Treaty of 1837. The Ojibwes were owed rations as well, from a similar treaty of their own. Taliaferro told the Ojibwes, including Hole in the Day's Gull River band and the villagers of St. Croix, that they had an agency of their own. The Chippewa Indian Agency was located at La Pointe, on the southwest tip of Lake Superior, more than two hundred miles away. Taliaferro gave them a small amount of rations and reluctantly allowed them to stay.

The Ojibwes and Dakotas had a hell of a good time together. They treated it as a sort of Olympics, with foot races, horse races and a ball game with eighty athletes per side. The leaders held a council, handing around the peace pipe. They agreed to refrain from warring for at least one year. There were signs of individual friendship and intimacy as well, including a romance between two young people, a Dakota warrior and an Ojibwe woman. After two weeks, Taliaferro coaxed the Ojibwes to be on their way, and the lovers wept as the woman left with her family.

Two of Hole in the Day's warriors were related to the man who had been killed at Cold Spring the previous August. On July 1, they hung back while the others headed north for home. Hole in the Day may have guessed the men's intentions. The pair went to their relative's grave to pay their respects. Later, in the dark of night, they approached the area of Man of the Sky's village and lay in wait on the opposite shore of Lake Harriet (south of Bde Maka Ska).

The next morning, Red Bird's nephew, Badger, who was also one of Man of the Sky's sons-in-law, went out at sunrise with his wife's little brother. In the village, five hundred souls went about their morning routine of "[h]unting, chopping, fishing, swimming, [and] playing." It was a day like any other, until:

> Suddenly, like a peal of thunder when no cloud is visible, here, there, everywhere, woke the startling alarm whoop, "Hoo, hoo, hoo!" Blankets were thrown in the air, men, women and children ran—they ran for life. Terror sat on every face—mothers grasped their little ones. All around was crying, wailing, shrieking, storming and scolding. Men vowed vengeance, whooped defiance, and dropped bullets into their gunbarrels. The excitement was intense and universal. The Chippewas! The Chippewas have surrounded us—we shall all be butchered!

They had discovered that Ojibwe warriors had shot Badger to death and scalped him. The assailants had been fast and quiet, but still Man of the Sky's son had seen them, and he ran home to raise the alarm. Red Bird scrambled to his nephew's side. He bent and kissed him. Badger's body

Lake Harriet, facing downtown. *Author's collection.*

Lake Harriet, southern shoreline. *Author's collection.*

was still warm, and his blood still ran. Red Bird cursed their enemies. Messengers went out to all the local Dakota villages. Within two hours, warriors assembled at the village, "painted, moccasined, victualated, and armed for the war path." Gideon Pond, recalling the event years later, remarked that "Indian warriors are all minute men."

The previous night, Big Thunder had hosted the St. Croix Ojibwes at Kaposia. Their guests had only just departed. Now, hours later, the Kaposian warriors armed themselves and applied war paint. Instead of attaching themselves to Red Bird's war party, they decided to pursue the St. Croix band. The Kaposian warriors took off in advance of Big Thunder, but in spite of his advanced age, he followed after them.

Red Bird's "avengers of blood" hailed from at least five other villages, in addition to the warriors from Bde Maka Ska. They agreed to reconvene at the base of the St. Anthony Falls. Pond did not note the path they took, but they may have carried their canoes south to the Minnehaha Creek and rowed east to its confluence with the Mississippi River, at the southeast corner of the Minnehaha Regional Park.

Minnehaha Creek at James Avenue S, about where Red Bird's warriors might have entered the creek, if that was their route to the Mississippi. *Author's collection.*

The warriors crossed the river and disembarked on the east bank, at modern-day Boom Island Park and B.F. Nelson Park and Main Street. From there, they carried their canoes over their heads as they proceeded down the slope to the falls' base. They would have walked by, or on, what is now Main Street. They came to a stop somewhere between the sites of Father Hennepin Bluff Park and the University of Minnesota Steam Plant.

The warriors lined up on the riverbank. If this were to happen today, then they would be visible from Main Street Southeast. Red Bird, nearly naked except for his paint, spoke an incantation to the sacred spirit as the three or four hundred warriors gave a collective wail. The medicine man handed the war pipe down the line, and he followed it. As he went, he "[lay] his hands on the head of each, binding him by all that is sacred in human relationships and religion" to strike their enemies.[18] Among his warriors was the lover of the young Ojibwe woman.

The next morning, July 3, the Kaposians caught up with their erstwhile St. Croix guests near Stillwater. The latter were recovering from a collective hangover after spending the prior evening carousing with some traders. The Kaposians waited for the whites to leave and then killed twenty-one Ojibwes and wounded twenty-nine. The Kaposians suffered very few casualties.

Meanwhile, Red Bird's men marched all through the night. By the Rum River, north of Anoka, they found the Gull River band. The Dakota warriors waited in ambush until the morning, when the Ojibwe warriors went in search of food. The remaining Ojibwe adults—old men, and women young and old—lifted onto their backs the bags of supplies that they carried for the trip. When they were thus burdened, the Dakotas fired on them.

The star-crossed young warrior led the rush to collect scalps. His lover ran to him with her wrists crossed to signify her surrender. He could not harm her, but he could not bring himself to betray Red Bird by helping her either. For the sake of appearances, he tapped her gently with the side of his spear and then ran. His brother-in-arms broke open her head with a tomahawk, to the crushing grief of the young man who really had loved her. He poured out his soul soon after the battle to a fur trader, telling him that he was so distraught that he wanted to die soon in battle. Fifty-six years later, that trader recalled in the *Pioneer Press* that the warrior got what he wanted.[19]

The Dakotas had not waited long enough before opening fire, and a party of Ojibwe warriors was still close enough to fight back, covering the vulnerable villagers' retreat. The Dakotas took the lives and scalps of seventy Ojibwes. Most of the casualties were women and children. The Ojibwe warriors fought back hard and killed Red Bird and his fifteen-year-old son, along with about a dozen other men.

Red Bird's warriors returned to Bde Maka Ska by nightfall. They first mourned their fallen. Man of the Sky and his fellows donned worn-out clothes, rubbed their faces with ashes and loosened their hair. The Kaposians brought their scalps to him, and they hung their collective ninety-one scalps from poles in the village center. They then performed a scalp dance, or, more accurately, the "Dance in Praise of One (who had taken the scalp)."[20] The villagers continued their dance for a month, and as they did so, they sang:

You Ojibwe, you are mean,
We will use you like a mouse,
We have got you and
We will strike you down,
My dog is very hungry,
I will give him the Ojibwe scalps.[21]

And *that* was the last scalp dance on the land of Minneapolis.

MAN OF THE SKY'S DECLINE

Historic Fort Snelling, the fortress itself, is located on Tower Avenue on the bluffs above the confluence of the Minnesota and Mississippi Rivers, a sacred spot which the Dakotas call "Bdote." The military reservation back then sprawled for miles around. If this description sounds irritatingly vague, that's because it is: the reservation borders were not formally mapped. The 1805 treaty with the Dakotas that granted the United States the land for the reservation did not specify the boundaries. Zebulon Pike, the young lieutenant who negotiated the treaty, had been ordered to explore the land along the Mississippi River that the Louisiana Purchase had delivered into the hands of the United States in 1803. His main objective had been to find the source of the Mississippi River. He erroneously identified it as Leech Lake instead of Lake Itaska. The "Pike Treaty" was also a blunder. Only a few chiefs showed up to his treaty council, not representative of all the villages who used the land for their hunting grounds. The text of the treaty included Pike's estimate that the land was worth $200,000, or more than $4,644,000 in modern currency.

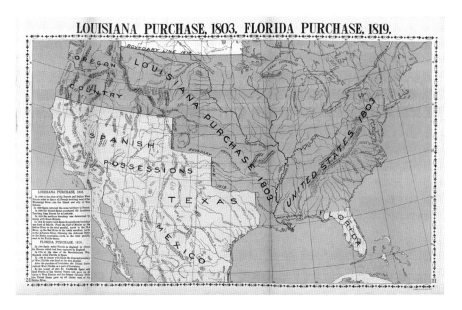

Above: Louisiana Purchase, 1803. Florida Purchase, 1819. *Library of Congress Geography and Map Division.*

Left: Promontory and lookout at Fort Snelling. *Hennepin County Library Digital Collections.*

Left: Fort Snelling from across the river. *Hennepin County Library Digital Collections*.

Below: Watch tower at Fort Snelling. *Hennepin County Library Digital Collections*.

Three years went by before the federal government took the treaty seriously. In 1808, the Senate, which was responsible for ratifying treaties, decided on the extent of the land. The reservation would extend 51,000 acres at the St. Croix River and more than 100,000 at Bdote. The Senate determined that the United States would pay $2,000 for all that land, not the $200,000 that Pike had anticipated. No Dakota chiefs were informed in advance of this or invited to negotiate the new specifications, and just like that, the Senate defrauded the Dakotas of nearly $4.6 million.

The Dakotas had their doubts about the land cessions, and they brought their concerns to Taliaferro. By May 1838, he had grown sick of their anxieties. He had advised them to sign the treaties, so of course the terms had been sound. He had assured the Dakotas that the U.S. government, the "Great Father," would keep its promises to them. He groused in his journal on the twenty-ninth of that month:

> *I find—by the talk of the Indians that they have been much worried on the subject of the Sales of their lands—that they would not be fulfilled—that their people thought they would be deceived—with many other idle stories.* [I am] *doomed to be annoyed by having to make frequent and repeated assurances of the good faith of the government.*

The wisdom and intuition of the Dakota leaders had exceeded Taliaferro's by leaps and bounds, and yet they had bowed to his imperious nature and signed the treaties. As the Dakotas had predicted, the government did not fulfill its treaty obligations. Taliaferro had strongly advised his "children" to accept the terms of the treaties, as he had not known that the U.S. commissioners were negotiating in bad faith, undervaluing the land just as the Senate had done after the 1820 treaty. The 1837 treaty had promised rations and then failed to convey them to Taliaferro on time, or they brought too little. The federal government had managed to both under-promise *and* under-deliver.

Taliaferro despaired. On July 15, 1839, at the age of forty-five, he tendered his resignation on the grounds of poor health. Maybe he was being honest and was experiencing stress-induced symptoms. Maybe he didn't want to mention that his "children," for whom he had advocated for nearly two decades, had lost faith in him after his government screwed them over, and that he had received death threats. Maybe he didn't want the War Department to know that he had been arrested as a co-conspirator in the arson of an east bank saloon that had been selling whiskey to his "children," whom he didn't trust to handle their drink.[22] The sheriff's deputy had handled him roughly, and Taliaferro—a child of privilege, an army major, an agent of the U.S. government and a former justice of the peace—was not used to such treatment.

He sought arrangements for Mary's room, board and education and took other steps to disengage. Man of the Sky heard rumors of this on August 8 and went with a few other leaders to see Taliaferro. They had chosen him to speak because of their familial connection. He told his son-in-law:

> [W]e know of no cause on our part why we should be discarded & left worse off than when we first heard the sound of your voice—a voice that gives us peace, plenty & good council and our children know it....[S]ay you will not desert us....We can never part with you; we had rather die than see you go off never to return back to us.

Taliaferro told him that he had already tendered his resignation and that it was too late to take it back. Man of the Sky was devastated to lose his son-in-law, and he thought of The Day Sets, who would lose her husband, and of Mary, who would lose her father. Taliaferro was family, and now he was leaving. They would miss him. It is not known today whether Mary saw her father again, but it appears that they corresponded and remained friends after his departure.

Plympton drew the Fort Snelling reservation boundary, a task that had been neglected until then. He made sure to include within it the area of the Bde Maka Ska village. He then "decided that he would have no Indian village inside the military reservation."[23] Man of the Sky wasn't going to fight it. Autumn came. He and his people harvested their crops for the last time and abandoned their home.

They relocated to Oak Grove, in what is now Bloomington. One of the advantages of that location, Man of the Sky had thought, was that it was more out of the way and less convenient for attackers. Hole in the Day was not deterred, and he did get his revenge.

The Dakotas, including Man of the Sky, eventually sold all their land. Nothing improved after Taliaferro's departure. The Dakota chiefs signed treaties under false promises by the federal government to pay their inflated debts to traders and to give them rations and pay cash that didn't arrive on time or in full. Man of the Sky saw his village deteriorating under the weight of alcoholism, communicable disease, interpersonal violence and suicide. He did all that he could to fight the decline, convinced that Christ would save them, that teetotalism would save them and that an American education would save them. He did what he could to impose his views in vain attempts to rescue his community, but he was grasping at straws and alienating the villagers with his fanaticism.

———

In the late morning of December 26, 1862, Man of the Sky and thirty-seven other Dakota leaders stood on a scaffold for their public execution, surrounded by thousands of hostile whites. Most of the other men at the gallows had participated in the Dakota War of 1862. They had massacred white settlers and taken up arms against the U.S. soldiers who came to the rescue. No historian of that era believes that Man of the Sky had any involvement in the violence. He wasn't the first or the last man, and not even the only man at the gallows that day, who was hanged for an act that he did not commit.

A "SORT OF FRENZY"

John Harrington Stevens was born in Québéc in 1820 but later moved to Wisconsin. In his late twenties, he served in the U.S. Army in the Mexican-American War. He fell ill and developed pulmonary dysfunction. A friend suggested to him that the "Wonderland of the Northwest," meaning what we now call the Upper Midwest, had a healthy climate for sufferers of respiratory illness.[24] Stevens accordingly traveled to St. Paul, where he quickly fell in love with the west bank, transfixed by the beauty of the prairies and especially by Minnehaha Falls. He got a job at the Fort Snelling sutler's store. Franklin Steele, the sutler, used his business connections to his employee's benefit. In 1849, Stevens was granted permission to settle on the Fort Snelling reservation, on the condition that he operate a ferry service on the Mississippi River. He built the first legal settler dwelling on the Minneapolis West Bank, between modern-day Hennepin Avenue Bridge and the Third Avenue Bridge. He had no white neighbors, aside from the soldiers and civilian employees of the fort, but he came to know the Natives. He frequently entertained, among many others, The Good Road and the young chiefs His Scarlet Nation, Big Thunder's son and Hole in the Day (the Younger).

Stevens's home, in which he raised his family, became known as the "birthplace of Minneapolis." He was called "Colonel Stevens," even

Right: Minnehaha Falls today. *Author's collection.*

Below: The old canteen and sutler's store at the rear of the guardhouse at Fort Snelling. *Hennepin County Library Digital Collections.*

Left: John H. Stevens, the first householder on the west bank of the Mississippi. *Hennepin County Library Digital Collections*.

Right: Statue of Colonel Stevens in front of the Stevens House. *Author's collection*.

Stevens House, now located in Minnehaha Park. It was moved there in 1896 and is now a museum. *Author's collection*.

though he had never achieved that rank in the army. It was merely a mark of respect for a town father who hosted councils between Native leaders and U.S. officials, and in whose living room Hennepin County and Minneapolis were formed.

Over time, as U.S. control over the region became more assured, the boundaries of the Fort Snelling reservation were expected to shrink, opening the land to white settlement. In a process called "preemption," the settlers could act immediately. If they flopped down on a patch of land, it was essentially theirs. The convention was that, later, they would have to purchase it from the government, but at bargain-basement prices. But they had to live there first. Real estate speculation nowadays can consist of buying up properties and land in as many places as you like, no matter where you live. Back then, your claim had to be your home or a place that you pretended was your home.

In the meantime, before that shrinkage, many prospective landowners were planning ahead. Most of them had no legal right to be there, as they were settling either on the military reservation or on Dakota land. The officials at Fort Snelling tolerated some squatters but not others. It was, and is, widely believed that substantial bribes to fort officials influenced their choice of who would get to stay. The fort issued permits to those allowed to reside on the reservation, and those without a permit were ordered off.

The Minnesota Territorial Assembly requested that the federal government reduce the thirty-four-thousand-acre reservation and extend preemption rights to west bank squatters. In 1852, Congress obliged and reduced the reservation to eight thousand acres, officially opening west bank land to white settlement. However, a stipulation of the act of Congress alarmed the squatters: the land would be sold at public auction. An auction? The vast majority of the squatters were small farmers. There was no way on earth that they would be able to outbid wealthy real estate investors. They had some time to ruminate, as the auction was scheduled for September 8, 1854.

Before a name was chosen sometime in the mid-1850s for the growing west bank town, its Ramsey County neighbors on the east bank bestowed on it the undeserved nickname "All Saints." The squatters, having already broken the law by settling, went on to break almost every tenet of the social contract. Hennepin County was incorporated that same year, three years after Stevens had settled by the river. He had already seen trouble among the settlers. They shamelessly jumped (that is, stole) one another's claims, either by taking advantage of their brief absences, or forcibly removing them. Men took their guns to bed with them in case of an attack during the night. They formed gangs for protection, and when they were compelled by necessity to step away from their claims, they traveled in packs for protection from rivals. At Stevens's famous house, he and his friends organized the Minnesota Protection Association.[25] This was one of several associations intended as a bulwark against "[a] sort of frenzy [that] seemed to possess people, which dulled all sense of honor, and led them to trample on the most sacred rights."[26]

Stevens had accurately predicted the settlement's future, as rivalry over claims intensified. Over "the next three years Hennepin county was a sort of battle-field."[27] Upcoming auction or no, men fought bitterly for their claims.

By 1855, all the land of Minneapolis had been divvied up into preemption claims. Minneapolis was still a year away from its incorporation as a township, yet it was already fully occupied, aside from land reserved for a school. What of the 1854 auction? It never happened, owing to a convenient bureaucratic mishap, and so Congress amended the original law to extend those preemption rights to all the squatters.

Even that did not bring peace. Part of the problem was that the law was complicated, and some of the would-be landowners did not understand its provisions or did not realize that every requirement in the law, no matter how small, was in fact *still required*. And worse, land sharks circled around the edges of future Minneapolis. They spied on settlers so closely that "[i]t was not safe to leave a pre-emption cabin unoccupied for ten minutes," because that was all the time that was needed for a claim jumper to hone in. The jumper "could be disloged only by personal violence, or by the payment of a sum of money." Greed was in the air, and even minnows turned into sharks: "Intimate friends and neighbors scrupled not to jump each others' claims, if they detected the slightest flaw in their satisfaction of the pre-emption law."[28]

The land office was located on Washington Avenue and Eighth Avenue South, now Washington Avenue South and Chicago Avenue in Downtown East, halfway between Mill Ruins Park to the north, and U.S. Bank Stadium to the south. Settlers, many of whom had brought their small children and banked their last asset on their claims, projected a quasi-mythic status on the land office.

A beautiful, verdant spring in 1856 brought the resolution of their claims, and the townspeople of Minneapolis sighed in relief—prematurely. They had accumulated debts while waiting patiently throughout the previous few years, and they attempted to satisfy them with mortgages. Some settlers had to sell their land at a fraction of its value, and many who labored day in and day out to pay off their mortgages found themselves ruined. Many families up and left, less than penniless. And yet the mill operators and manufacturers moved in for the waterpower of the falls, and hoteliers and retailers set up shop to accommodate them. As always, the wealthy thrived, while the poor barely survived. There is one bright note to this troubled era: most of the families who were forced away by their poverty returned over the years, drawn once again to the beauty of the land that they had once tended with such hope.

PART II
EARLY MINNEAPOLIS

A COLD(-HEARTED) JUNE

There was no concert that Thursday night, but a crowd had gathered inside Barber's Hall at the corner of Second Avenue South and Washington Avenue, about four blocks west of the Hennepin Avenue Bridge. It was June 17, 1856, and the week before had been a frightening one. It had been *cold*. The frigid weather didn't damage the crops, but Minneapolitans and the rest of the Hennepin County settlers reassembled the stoves that they had set aside for the summer and lit their fires. None of them had ever felt such cold during the month of June as they did on the thirteenth of that month.[29] But it wasn't the shocking weather that had drawn the crowd. They had come to talk about the murders.

Earlier that week, on June 11, Mr. John A. Hathaway left his cabin on the bank of Crow River, in modern-day Rogers in northwest Hennepin County. Hathaway's wife, Mary Jane, and their fourteen-month-old child stayed home while he went out to tend to the crops, far enough away that he was out of sight and earshot of his family.

When he came home for dinner, he found his wife lying on the floor, with their fourteen-month-old next to her—playing in her blood. The victim had been shot in the head with a pistol. Aside from the toddler, there were no witnesses. Mrs. Hathaway had been a respected member of the community, and there was no clear motive for the crime. This was the first murder ever committed in Hennepin County.

On the same day as Mrs. Hathaway's murder, a small group of Ojibwes came to the Whallen home to "beg." Asking strangers for food did not carry the same negative connotations for them as it did for the settlers. Like Man of the Sky, Ojibwes reflexively shared with those who had less than them. Throughout the earliest years of white settlement, the Objibwes and the Dakotas had shared their food and shelter with settlers who otherwise would have perished. Right now, the Ojibwes had less, and the whites had more. Treaties with the United States were gnawing away at Ojibwe lands to the north, and so the people who lived there had to wander far from home to find sufficient food. That was what brought them south to Oak Grove, where the Whallens lived, on land that Man of the Sky and his villagers had briefly called home.

While they were at the Whallens' house, the Ojibwe "beggars" saw young Susan, a Dakota child. Because the Dakotas of southwest Minnesota were in terrible shape, a lot of parents asked settlers to foster their children and raise them in the American fashion, which appeared to be ascendant. Susan's Kaposian family had sent her to live with the Whallen family when she was five or six years old. Now ten years old, she was thoroughly assimilated. The only marker of her heritage was her face itself.

The next day, June 12, Mrs. M. S. Whallen was entertaining their neighbor, Mrs. Ames. The women were in the sitting room with Susan and two other children. Three or four Ojibwe men entered the room, unannounced and armed. They dragged ten-year-old Susan out of the house, slit her throat and scalped her. The men were fast at their slaughter, and they were not caught at the scene.

Mrs. Hathaway and Susan had been murdered within two days of each other. The settlers were outraged. A theory circulated that they had the same killers. It was possible. Assuming that the Ojibwe men who killed Susan had been the same ones who came to the Whallen home the day before, they would have had to travel about thirty miles, the distance from the Hathaway home to Oak Grove. Both homes were close to the riverbank, and the men could have been going up and down the river, stopping at settlements to ask for food. Maybe they killed Mrs. Hathaway in anger because she hadn't given them as much as they needed. There is the lingering issue of the differing M.O.s, however.

Whoever it was who did it, the clamoring citizens at Barber's Hall wanted justice for these innocent victims. John H. Stevens drafted a resolution, which an appointed committee of community leaders unanimously adopted:

This county, for the first time in its history has, during the past week, been visited with wilful and malicious murders, attended by a barberous and fiendish spirit, which call loudly for a decided expression of the sentiment of the people; that it is the duty of every law-abiding citizen and every lover of justice, to use his utmost endeavor to bring the perpetrators of these foul crimes to punishment; that while we cannot restore the lost lives, or blot out the outrages that have been inflicted upon individuals, or the wrongs to their families and citizens generally, we can and will take measures to punish the guilty; that we have full confidence in the power of the civil authorities to impartially administer the laws, and to legally punish all crimes; that we deprecate any attempt on the part of individuals to resort to violence, or to take the execution of the law into their own hands. [30]

There were two more murders shortly after that, and then, for years to come, there were no more murders among the settlers of Hennepin County. Thirty-three years after the Barber's Hall meeting, Stevens wrote, "None of the murderers have been apprehended or brought to justice, and probably they never will be." [31]

ESCAPE FROM CHRISTMAS

Mrs. Eliza O. Winston hovered anxiously in the woods behind a house on Lake Harriet. Her captors had sent her back there, and one of them kept checking on her to make sure she stayed out of sight. Rescue was on the way, Mrs. Winston was sure of it. She had made contact with a St. Antonian woman and had told her that "she wanted to be free and was held against her will." [32]

Minneapolis is very proud of its progressive reputation. Our city is "Strongly Liberal." [33] According to *Forbes*, we were the sixth-most liberal U.S. city in 2015. [34] We "rank well" in urban diversity. [35] Minnesota never had an anti-miscegenation law, which would have banned racial intermarriage. It was also never a slave state. There were slaveholders here, way back at the beginning, before the state was born. They were soldiers at Fort Snelling, coming from the South, like Taliaferro, and bringing their unpaid servants with them.

But there was still an informal trade among them. In addition to Taliaferro loaning out the unfortunate people whom he "owned," northerners like the Massachusetts-born Colonel Snelling faced little difficulty purchasing them from the southern officers.

Thanks to a strong abolitionist contingent, there was no question of Minnesota becoming a formal slave state. The immigrant pioneers, fresh from Scandinavia, Ireland and Germany, hadn't been in the United States long enough to develop a tolerance to the concept of human bondage. Regardless, when the time came to elect officers to a state constitutional referendum, ordered for October 13, 1857, only those who met the criteria of "free white male inhabitant of full age, who should have resided in the state for ten days before the election, [were] authorized to vote."[36]

Earlier that year, in the spring of 1857, twenty-one-year-old Emily O.G. Grey brought her toddler, William, to St. Anthony (which would later merge with Minneapolis and become St. Anthony West). Her husband had arrived first, in 1855, to carve out a niche for their family after William's birth. Mr. Grey had set up a barbershop in the Jarrett House, a hotel on Main Street. Mrs. Grey's father had been a barber, too, after he was freed from slavery in 1821. As for her, she was a lively, compassionate woman, with a big personality to match her large build. She would have been imposing if she weren't so kind. She was so fair-skinned that she had visible freckles, and she had blue-gray eyes. Back home, in York, Pennsylvania, her dad was busy helping runaway slaves and hosting abolitionist meetings. He was such a force to be reckoned with that, in six years' time, Confederate forces would head to York in hopes of capturing him.

The Greys were not the first Black family in the Minneapolis/St. Anthony area, but it was a small group that they joined. The white residents were generally friendly, and Mr. and Mrs. Grey were members of civic organizations. Mr. Grey, of course, as a nonwhite resident, was excluded from the suffrage, but although he was unable to vote, he was vocal and eloquent in his opinions. He was persuasive and powerful in his own way, as well as a good friend of Frederick Douglass. In 1873, Grey would host that great man when he came to Minnesota.

Despite the fact that Grey, and some freemen like him, owned successful businesses and participated actively in the community, the voters of Minnesota did not feel the need to allow all Black Americans the same

St. Anthony along Lower Main Street in 1857. *Hennepin County Library Digital Collections.*

St. Anthony from the Winslow House, looking northeast. *Hennepin County Library Digital Collections.*

St. Anthony from the roof of the Winslow House Hotel. *Hennepin County Library Digital.*

opportunities. Six months after Mrs. Grey's arrival, "[t]he [pro-slavery] Democrats obtained a majority of the legislators and nearly all the state and national offices" at the state constitutional convention.[37] There were many Minnesotans who were not so hostile to the idea of keeping humans in captivity. It wasn't only deep-seated political beliefs that made them okay with this: it was also tourist dollars.

It may surprise some readers to know that tourism was a thriving industry in Minneapolis and St. Anthony in the 1850s. Tourists came for the nature, the Falls of St. Anthony, Minnehaha Falls, rolling prairie and sparkling lakes. There were riverboat tours and lakeside picnics. There were day trips out to the tamed wilderness at the edges of Hennepin and Ramsey Counties. Most importantly for the southern gentry, there was a refreshing lack of malaria, and they traveled up the Mississippi River in droves during summertime. In 1856, the Winslow House was built on a hill overlooking Main Street, very close to the Jarrett House. It was built with southern tourists in mind, in a Colonial Revival architectural style. "[Q]uite a pretentious structure[,]" in Mrs. Grey's words.[38] The Winslow was a luxurious place, with two hundred rooms on six stories as well as a croquet lawn. Because of the hotel's height and location, its roof was an excellent vantage point, and photographers brought their cameras up there to capture views of the cities of Minneapolis and St. Anthony.

Winslow House Hotel in St. Anthony. *Hennepin County Library Digital Collections.*

Main Street, St. Anthony. *Hennepin County Library Digital Collections.*

The timing of the Winslow House construction could not have been better from a business perspective. In March 1857, shortly before Mrs. Grey's arrival in St. Anthony, the U.S. Supreme Court handed down its decision in the *Dred Scott v. Sandford* case. It had been nineteen years since Taliaferro had officiated the marriage of Mr. and Mrs. Scott. They and their two daughters had been loaned out, transferred, sent and summoned all over the lands of the Louisiana Purchase. The Scotts sued for freedom, mostly on the basis of the substantial time that they had spent in free states.[39] The Supreme Court ruled against the Scott family, arguing that granting them freedom on this basis would violate their captor's property rights.

After the court case, Sanford[40] sold the Scotts to a man with a conscience, who freed them. Mr. Scott succumbed to tuberculosis within the year. He was born in captivity and lived in captivity, but he died a freeman. His case would have implications for all men and women with the same dream that the Scott family had had.

It certainly bolstered the confidence of wealthy southern tourists, who knew now that they could travel north with the people they "owned" without interference from local abolitionists. Minneapolis/St. Anthony was a particularly safe location, far enough north to beat the southern heat but not so far north as to allow for convenient access to the Canadian border— once an enslaved person crossed the border, he or she was free. For all these reasons, Christmas came to St. Anthony.

In August 1860, Colonel Richard Christmas took the river north from Issaquena, Mississippi, with his wife, Mary; their five-year-old daughter, Norma; and an enslaved servant woman, thirty-year-old Eliza O. Winston. They were staying at the Winslow House when Mrs. Winston sought out Mrs. Grey for help.

On the twenty-first of that month, Mrs. Grey and two of her friends "joined in a petition to the district court, setting forth that Mrs. Winston was unlawfully deprived of her liberty…and demanding the release of the slave woman."[41] The district court judge, thirty-three-year-old Yale alumnus Charles E. Vanderburgh, issued a writ of habeas corpus. This is an order to law enforcement to bring an individual to the court. It is usually associated with compelling a defendant to appear for prosecution, but it can also be used to bring in witnesses as well. This was the case for Mrs. Winston.

Sheriff Strout went to the Winslow House to serve the writ, but Christmas, who had been tipped off, moved his family to a house on Lake Harriet, where they were now staying as guests. When Strout got there, the Christmas family tried at first to keep Mrs. Winston, but they knew that tangling with law enforcement would be an exercise in futility. In the end, other than attempting to emotionally manipulate her into staying, they did not interfere with her departure.

Strout brought Mrs. Winston to the courthouse. She had an advocate there, and she also gave an eloquent deposition. Vanderburgh ignored the *Dred Scott* precedent and ruled that as Mrs. Winston was "being held as a slave in the free state of Minnesota, clearly in violation of the law…[she] was granted her liberty."[42]

There was vicious anger in Minneapolis and St. Anthony. According to a historian of the era, there was talk of "lynching those who were concerned in procuring the poor woman's freedom."[43] Many of the native-born whites in the cities were proslavery, and some others who didn't take a side on the issue of freedom were still in a lather over the potential loss of tourism if southern travelers were to start avoiding the area.

Mrs. Winston exited the courthouse through the backdoor, into a circle of supporters. On the front steps, a crowd had formed with the intention of kidnapping her and returning her to Christmas. The colonel persuaded them that he did not desire this. He was fond of Mrs. Winston and believed that she was fond of him too. He did not want her brought back by force. He was convinced that she would come back to him and his family of her own accord.

That night, one of the petitioners, either Mrs. Grey or her abolitionist friend, Mr. Babbitt, sheltered Mrs. Winston in their home. A mob of about twenty men, led by the owner of the Winslow Hotel, formed outside "to tar and feather [the householder] and possibly to recover [Mrs. Winston]."[44] The sky opened, as if in anger at the crowd, and poured out rain on them. As if that wasn't discouraging enough, they heard a pistol shot inside the house. That sent the last of the cowardly fools running.

Within forty-eight hours of Vanderburgh's ruling, the Underground Railroad had spirited Mrs. Winston away, toward the Canadian border.

The local Democratic press sided with the violent mob. As a shining example, the *Weekly Pioneer and Democrat* came unhinged that day. A special correspondent, in an August 24 article titled "The Hennepin County Slave Case—Triumph of the 'Freedom Shriekers,'" referred to the rescue of Mrs. Winston as "n----r stealing," wrote smugly of a bad scare that the mob had given to Mr. Babbitt, issued thinly veiled threats against Mr. Grey's safety and Vanderburgh's job. Another article on the same page celebrated the "wholesome thrashing" that a tourist from Mississippi had given to a "meddling and insulting Abolitionist" in the wake of the Winston case. It was like a racist bingo card. Further afield, some Democratic newspapers were appalled by this grotesque pandering. The *St. Cloud Democrat* referred to the would-be kidnappers as "dirt-eaters" and "toadies" and spoke in respectful terms of Mrs. Winston and her St. Antonian friends.[45]

Local Republican newspapers "took pains to insist that their party had taken no part in the transaction and was not responsible for it....They... deprecated interference with the servants of southern visitors." But at least one paper, the *Weekly Express* of St. Anthony, was honest about its motives: it feared the damage to the tourist industry. The *Weekly Pioneer* groused, "The boats took down yesterday a large number of southern visitors, and the Abolitionists have 'accomplished their perfect work.'"

Everyone would eventually get what they deserved.

Vanderburgh's rulings did not harm his popularity with the electorate. Reelections kept him in the district court until 1880. His determination to exercise his own judgment won him respect in the young state of Minnesota, and he was considered a trailblazer. He was elected associate justice of the Minnesota Supreme Court, where he found a home for twelve years before he decided to return to practicing law.

Mrs. Grey would go on to become a *grande dame* of St. Antonian society, and Mr. Grey would hold a place of equal stature. Their second child, Toussaint l'Ouverture Grey, was the first Black child born in St. Anthony.

The Winslow House, ironically, became a casualty of its own practice of catering to slaveholders. The hotel was so dependent on those southerners that when tourist traffic from below the Mason-Dixon line dried up during the Civil War, the hotel was stripped for parts. The furniture was taken out in 1861, and the Winslow House ceased to be a hotel in 1872. The building itself was razed in 1886.

THE BRIDGE SQUARE FIRES

One June 9, 1860, a fire broke out in a small building on Bridge Square in Minneapolis. Two- and three-story frame buildings for homes and offices lined the north and south sides of the square, which started from the bank of the river, where Hennepin Avenue and Nicollet Avenue end, and ran up to the block where Hennepin Avenue, Washington Avenue, Nicollet Avenue and Third Street South come together. This is the core of the present-day Gateway District. There stood the Nicollet House, a fashionable hotel that was only two years old. Bridge Square was the retail hub of Minneapolis, and the city couldn't afford to lose it. Too bad it didn't have a fire department.

Bridge Square, looking down Third Street. *Hennepin County Library Digital Collections.*

Good thing St. Anthony had one. The Minnesota Engine Company and the Cataract Engine Company, both of St. Anthony, managed to extinguish the fire with the help of the locals. They had to drain the miniature lake in the square to do it, and this source was all used up within thirty minutes. It was believed that the cause was arson.

Nine days later, on June 18, Bridge Square caught fire once again, and it wasn't just one building this time. The arsonist, who was never caught, started the fire in a store on the frame row on the north side of the square. The fire department of St. Anthony drained its station houses, sending all of its men across the river. By the time they got there, the fire had destroyed eighteen buildings, rendering businesses without offices and families without homes. The fire department didn't have enough hose to make it from the river to the square. Three fire engines had to function as hoses, feeding water from one to the next in a row, to add length, and an ad hoc Minneapolitan bucket brigade chipped in as well. Nobody died, but it was starting to dawn on Minneapolis that it couldn't rely on St. Anthony's fire services forever.

PART III

DARK SATANIC MILLS

The Falls Collapse

"There was no need of a prophet to foretell the establishment of great industries at the Falls of St. Anthony," wrote William Watts Folwell, the first president of the University of Minnesota.[46] It started with lumber. Stunning pine forests, said to be the most beautiful on earth, constituted a large area of Ojibwe hunting grounds. That wood made great lumber. The lumber companies lied, cheated and stole the land out from underneath the locals, and corrupt American officials facilitated their fraud. The mills were ever hungry for more lumber, and those gorgeous pinelands vanished, while the Ojibwes starved from the loss of their traditional food sources in the forests. Government rations were not only insufficient to make up the difference, but they were also unreliable.[47]

But there was nothing unreliable about the power of the St. Anthony Falls. Flour mills and sawmills had provided food and building materials to the soldiers of Fort Snelling and, later, to the settlers. In 1855, the St. Anthony Falls Water Power Company set up operations on the east bank of the falls. The next year, the Minneapolis Mill Company mirrored it across the falls. The year after that, in 1857, construction began on a canal on the west side of the Mississippi. After this, more mills came up. The year 1865 brought an extension of the canal and, with it, the great, hulking flour mills that made the Mill City what it is. Supporting

St. Anthony Falls seen from the West Bank. *Hennepin County Library Digital Collections*.

industries popped up around the falls in metal works, wood works and other manufactory.

Many Minnesotan settlers, including Folwell, deplored the poor condition of Ojibwe communities and the avaricious collusions of businessmen and U.S. officials that had brought it about. Although some settlers didn't know, many knew and simply didn't care. They figured that all that suffering other people endured was worth if it meant that the mills could thrive. This industry was only hurting Natives—the Dakotas, who had been pushed far, far from home to make way for the cities and their mills, and the Ojibwes, who suffered death by a thousand cuts. It would never harm the grand mill cities of Minneapolis and St. Anthony.

The Falls of St. Anthony were sacred to the Dakotas, and European explorers and pioneers had once raved of their beauty in prose and poetry. There was another element of the falls that had attracted the attention of intrepid adventurers: waterpower. In the 1800s, the rights to waterpower were held by the owner of land upriver by the generator of the power—in this case, the falls.

The Minneapolis Mill Company and the St. Anthony Falls Water Power Company together controlled the waterpower that the falls generated. They expected to be in business forever, on an eternal gravy train. All they had to do was maintain their canals and their fifteen-foot-high dams. Those dams narrowed the channel, as did debris from the mills. So fully did they commit to their duopoly that they built millponds, one by the west bank and one by the east bank, to ensure that the water was evenly diverted to, and divided between, the two companies. Below the riverbed of silt and sand, the upper

St. Anthony Falls from the west side, 1860s. *Hennepin County Library Digital Collections.*

Old government mills at St. Anthony Falls. *Hennepin County Library Digital Collections.*

stratum of the bedrock was limestone, which already is not the sturdiest of surfaces. Below it lay sandstone that was more than 99.4 percent pure silica, which the historian John O. Anfinson characterized as the "'Ivory Soap' of sandstone."[48] Carving out the millponds exposed to freezing temperatures parts of the bedrock that had never before seen the light of day or felt so much as a breeze. Nature was both more fragile, and more determined, than the mill companies realized.

Erosion had been wearing away at the St. Anthony Falls for eight thousand years, moving them farther and farther upriver. Minneapolitans and St. Antonians didn't much care that the waterfall was receding faster now, with the man-made changes to the river altering its course and pressure. The water was hitting the cliff of the falls from directions and at speeds that nature had not designed it to handle. St. Paulites had more distance, and they could see the danger. Their newspapers reported on the risk to the waterfall, but the cities of industry treated their warnings as an attempt at malicious harm. It was "atrocious slander," said the *Minneapolis Tribune*, on September 27, 1866, and it would cause Minneapolis and St. Anthony "incalculable injury." To prevent such injury, "no pains should be spared to acquaint the public with the truth." By "injury," the *Tribune* meant withdrawal of investment in Minneapolis/St. Anthony's milling industries, and by "truth" it meant that there was no harm in the falls' recession.

It was no wonder that the press, or its backers, was so eager to suppress naysayers. "The Mississippi River and St. Anthony Falls were everything" to early Minneapolis and St. Anthony.[49] Their economy could not survive without the waterpower from the falls. Those cities were nothing without their mills, but no brainwashing could erase the evidence. People who lived and worked near the falls began to notice that they were wearing away so quickly that they could see the falls move back from one year to the next. They could see the limestone breaking off, bit by bit, and crashing down with the water. In 1866, the Minneapolis Mill Company shelled out $25,000 (about $423,000 today) for an apron. It contracted former employee and civil engineer Franklin Cook to construct it.

Cook placed a protective covering of planks and timbers over the falls and weighted it down with rocks. Onlookers mourned the loss of the falls' beauty. At least they could all rest easy now, knowing that the recession had come to an end. The next year, the river rose sixteen feet higher than usual, and in the flood, the falls tore off the apron.

By 1868, the citizens of both mill cities had grown anxious. They could see all too clearly that the falls couldn't last long without intervention. The

St. Anthony Falls just after the construction of the first apron. *Hennepin County Library Digital Collections.*

problem was: who should pay for it? The federal and Minnesota state governments said that it was the responsibility of the cities of Minneapolis and St. Anthony. The citizens there disagreed and said that it was the mills' problem. The Minneapolis Mill Company had already paid for the first apron, and it didn't have another $25,000 lying around that it could throw at another one. And rival mill owner William Wallace Eastman was about to launch a separate assault on the falls.

EASTMAN WAS BORN IN Conway, New Hampshire, in 1827, the third of eight children. His family had lived in New England ever since the colonial era. In his youth, he worked in his dad's paper mill and drove a stagecoach. He was highly educated, having attended the South Conway seminary. After finishing his education, he headed west. He went to San Francisco by ship but fell ill on his journey. His sickness soured him on the city, and he stayed only two weeks before going back to his family. He continued to live with them for a number of years. In 1854, he came to St. Anthony, where he reunited with an elder brother, John Whittemore Eastman, who was a partner in the Minnesota Flouring Mill on the east side of Hennepin Island. William soon became a partner too.

In 1858, after four years of working with John, thirty-one-year-old William was ready to strike out on his own. He sold out and went into business with Paris Gibson. They built the Cataract Mill, the first west bank flour mill. That was a huge success, and soon they added the North Star woolen mills to its west bank collection. William Eastman would hop from one partnership to another after that, always the leader and innovator.

In 1865, William Eastman and his current partners purchased the forty-acre Nicollet Island, slightly upriver of the St. Anthony Falls. Eastman planned to turn the southern half of the island into an industrial center, with mills and factories. Eastman intended to take advantage of the water rights conventions to operate his yet-to-be-built mill on Nicollet Island without paying the duopoly. He and his associates sued the St. Anthony Milling Company on the grounds that the sawmills on the east bank ran on waterpower that rightfully belonged to the Nicollet Island business. The St. Anthony Company was alarmed. To make the lawsuit go away and not risk its mills, it compromised.

Their 1867 agreement permitted a Looney Tunes–esque solution to Eastman's problem of how to get sufficient waterpower farther upstream from the waterfall: burrowing under the river, directly beneath the falls. Upriver of the falls, a headrace tunnel would reroute water into a 30-foot drop shaft. As the water poured out from it, it would generate two hundred horsepower for the mills and factories that Eastman expected to build south of the Hennepin Avenue Bridge. Then, having done that, the water would go out a 2,500-foot-long, 6-by-6-foot tailrace tunnel. At the end of the tailrace, which would open immediately downriver of Hennepin Island, the water would rush out. The tunnel would snake deep underneath the St. Anthony Falls, the ceiling of Hennepin Island and all the rest of the St. Anthony Company's sawmill operations and millpond, without disrupting the activities of that company. There were already about five hundred similar, smaller tunnels under the Mississippi River. There were successful models for what came to be known as "Eastman's Tunnel," but never before had it been attempted on such a scale. Work started on the tunnel on September 7, 1868.

East Side Lumber Mills. *Hennepin County Library Digital Collections.*

A FEW YEARS BEFORE that project, Eastman and his companies assisted a pair of cousins in the development of a firefighting service. George A. Brackett had been twenty years old when he left his home state of Maine in 1856. Despite his youth and low education relative to the other town fathers, he quickly distinguished himself among them as one of the city's first aldermen. When he first came to St. Anthony, he worked for a butcher. Then he owned his own company. Then he became president of the Minneapolis Stockyards. He was the contracted beef supplier to the Minnesota troops deployed up north in the Dakota War.

He got into milling and became a partner with Eastman, Gibson & Company. In 1865, his cousin, twenty-two-year-old Winslow M. Brackett,

Left: George A. Brackett. *Hennepin County Library Digital Collections*.

Right: Winslow Brackett. *Hennepin County Library Digital Collections*.

came to town after serving for three years in the Union army. George got Winslow a job as a bookkeeper with the Eastman company. Winslow was one of nature's bookkeepers, with an eye for discrepancies. He had been a hoseman with a fire department in his home state of Maine prior to the war. Winslow was in Minneapolis for a matter of months before he realized that the fire services that existed in the city at that time would not suffice to meet the needs of the growing mill district. Winslow founded the firefighting Millers' Association, and its ranks were filled mostly with the employees of the flour mills. Eastman's businesses supplied the hardware—Eastman, Gibson & Company owned five hundred feet of hose, and the water to put out fires came from the rotary pump in the basement of the Cataract Mill.

Three years later, in January 1868, the Minneapolis City Council organized a volunteer firefighting force, divided into three companies. Residents of the mill district had chipped in to buy the uniforms. One week after that, at a meeting of all the companies, George Brackett was chosen to be chief engineer.

IT WAS AROUND THAT same time that Franklin Cook and the citizens of Minneapolis and St. Anthony succeeded in getting the state legislature to issue bonds to raise the money for another apron over the falls. The bond bill compelled the mill companies to give $5,000 for every $20,000 that the cities issued in bonds. The companies also committed to covering any additional operating costs to maintain the St. Anthony Falls. The city voters approved the bond issues in early spring of 1869.

The *Minneapolis Tribune* effused breathlessly:

> *Our waterpower is no longer in danger, for our citizens, with the characteristic energy which builds up the great cities of the mighty West, have resolved to meet and oppose the destructive powers of nature herself, and they know the cunning handiwork that will stay her ceaseless forces and turn them into channels of industry and make them the servants of man!*

Minneapolis would be better, bigger, than the great mill city of Lowell, Massachusetts, the *Tribune* predicted. The article could have been trifolded and used as a brochure for recruiting investors: "Let all who have capital, or skill, or labor to invest…make haste to locate in a city of enterprise, public spirit, and in material advantages without a peer."[50] The future could not have been brighter for Minneapolis.

Construction on the new apron began in midsummer. Massive crews, at times numbering one hundred men, worked on the apron. The *Tribune* squealed with joy along the way. By September 1869, the crew had made good progress, but "heavy rains swelled the river…raging waters reached the falls… [and] hundreds of logs crashed over the new apron."[51] Construction halted.

While Cook and company were busy with the topside of the falls, William Eastman's tunneling crew was hard at work underneath them. The workers had started at Hennepin Island. The first thing they did was to construct a staircase from ground level down into a tunnel. Over the next year, they built the tunnel far up under the falls. By the autumn of 1869, the men had reached the downriver edge of Nicollet Island. The end was in sight, metaphorically speaking.

On the morning of October 4, 1869, the crew was at work underneath the south end of Nicollet Island, the tunnel almost complete. On October 4, 1869, the crew was at work on the south end of Nicollet Island, the tunnel almost complete. Water started trickling down into the tunnel. The workmen were no cowards, digging away under the mighty Mississippi, but they knew immediately that it wasn't worth the risk to keep going. They stuck it out until noon and then packed up and scrambled down along the tunnel, under the falls. They escaped up the staircase on Hennepin Island. By some miracle, they had all cleared the tunnel before it began "spouting a volume of water which rushed through it at a terrific velocity."[52] The source of the tunnel leak could not be located. Later, it was found that the limestone base of Nicollet Island had fallen in, on top of the fragile sandstone beneath it, and the walls of the tunnel beneath that. A sinkhole more than ninety feet across and sixteen feet deep had formed in the sandstone underneath the southern tip of the island.

By the next morning, October 5, a powerful whirlpool had formed close to Nicollet Island, about two hundred feet below the Hennepin Avenue Bridge and more than five hundred feet away from the tunnel. A bystander remarked that the volume of water that the whirlpool poured into the tunnel rivaled the entire Rum River. To the average citizen watching on the shore, this would have been bizarre and alarming. Those who fully understood the wear and tear that the mills had caused the limestone bedrock and the sandstone beneath it knew that "the erosion of this volume of water would soon undermine the limestone bed of the river, which, falling in, would ruin the falls and replace them by a series of rapids."[53]

The east bank "mills along the riverfront were sucked into this vortex, carried through the enlarged tunnel, and spat out" of the downriver tunnel opening, where it slammed the southern part of Hennepin Island, snapping off a 150-foot triangle of land.[54] The Minneapolis firefighters had just finished putting out a fire, and so the men were already mobilized. An alarm was sounded, and they ran to Hennepin Island. Minneapolitans and St. Antonians flocked to the island or watched from the riverbanks or bridges. Hundreds of men ran down to help salvage whatever they could from the mills on Hennepin Island.

Underneath one of the crews, the land caved in. The men were saved, but much of the island was lost as "the battering waters [tore] Hennepin Island to pieces, rolling great rocks into the stream as though they were shavings."[55] The river crested the east bank, flooding St. Anthony. George Brackett shrugged off his elegant suit jacket. "That water *must* be stopped."[56] He ran through the crowd, drumming up support. John Jarvis, a yardmaster with the Milwaukee and St. Paul Railroad, rolled up his sleeves. "Boys, let's plug that hole." Jack Tid, a local celebrity, joined in. The three ringleaders directed the thousands of volunteers who came to help the firefighters. The mills sent out their workers to join the effort, working away at the sinkhole on Nicollet Island. They chucked everything they could find into the hole to plug it. They dropped in stones, felled trees, logs and various debris, but to no avail. Their fillings were "tossed around, thrown up in the air and then drawn down out of sight by a force that snapped them off like pipe stems."[57]

The men didn't back down. They built a raft out of a pile of timbers that had been left on the island. The same types of things that they had previously thrown into the hole they now put on the raft to weigh it down. When they had finished loading, the raft's contents were piled several feet high. The men then set it over the sinkhole, where it floated in the water and then settled into place. They did it! They plugged the hole! Some of the men were still standing on the raft, while others strutted at the bank of the island, arms thrown up to the sky, while they gazed out in triumph at their vanquished foe, "which seemed to be snarling in defeat."[58]

Then the center of the raft dropped. The men standing on that part of the raft feared for their lives, but the center rose once more and the men scrambled for land. The raft was merely a sieve now, with no impact on the water flow. It sank out of sight. The workers realized, then, that it was not enough to plug holes. They worked until morning, by the light of lanterns and bonfires, constructing dams near the hole to divert water away from the damaged area of bedrock and dropping sandbags and trees into the sinkhole on the island. Throughout the following day, October 6, they sank several rafts, each piled with rocks, into the whirlpool. Yet the water continued its surge down the tunnel under the falls.

Increasingly complex and effective measures were implemented over the coming weeks. Reporters from all over the country flocked to the mill

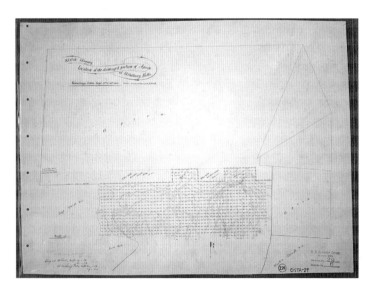

Sketch showing the location of the damaged portion of the apron at St. Anthony Falls. *Hennepin County Library Digital Collections.*

cities of the Northwest. The *Minneapolis Daily Tribune* was frantic to dismiss the negative publicity. The paper argued that there was no "occasion for alarm." Sadly, because it sought to minimize the danger and the damage, the paper downplayed the heroism of the volunteers. It was the out-of-town reporters who recorded the words and actions of men like Brackett who salvaged Nicollet and Hennepin Islands. But even the aggressively optimistic *Tribune* couldn't pretend that this would be a permanent solution: according to it, the volunteers' stopgap "might and probably would resist abrasion…for a month, or for a period indefinitely longer, and perhaps, would endure for years."[59]

It was looking bleak for the mill cities. The repairs had been, and would continue to be, expensive. In Minneapolis and St. Anthony, citizens formed the Union Committee for Falls Preservation. They raised $22,000 (about $435,000 today) and expected the mill companies to pay it back. Eastman's company was assessed less than the Minneapolis Mill and St. Anthony companies and the cities of Minneapolis and St. Anthony. The only assessees who would pay less than Eastman and his fellows were two Hennepin Island manufacturers. Litigation over this distribution of responsibility ensued, delaying construction.

Before too long, the river broke through the dam and coursed down the tunnel. The sandstone continued its accelerated erosion. Six months later, in April 1870, the river flooded. It was too much for the limestone ceiling on Hennepin Island's northern bank, and it fell in. The resulting sinkhole took out some of the St. Anthony Milling Company's sawmills. That company, and not Eastman's, filled the sinkholes.

It took nearly a year after the initial tunnel break to persuade the federal government to send out the Army Corps of Engineers. It was the cities' problem, federal officials first told them. Then the cities changed tack. Instead of wringing their hands about the loss of their industry, the supplicants requested aid on the grounds that if the falls were destroyed, giving way to rapids and sinkholes, transportation by river would be impeded, and that, in turn, would pose a risk to national security. The Indian Wars were in full swing. Access up and down, as well as across, the Mississippi was essential to the war effort.

The measures the corps would undertake would balloon in both intensity and expense. At one point, Minneapolis and St. Anthony requested $200,000 (nearly $4 million today). It was a hard-fought battle. They built a dam, but the sandstone continued breaking. They shored up the limestone on the falls with an earthen apron and the banks with earthen ramparts. In April 1873,

View of Minneapolis, west side mills from roof of Winslow House. The area in the foreground appears to be flooded. *Hennepin County Library Digital Collections.*

the river broke through the dam, swept away a large part of the embankment and knocked a 150-foot hole in the wall, killing a man. Eastman now had blood on his hands.

The St. Anthony Falls ended up needing a concrete apron, which we still have today. In addition to that, the corps had to build two dams and a sluiceway to regulate the river and make it more convenient for industry. It was too late for the St. Anthony Milling Company. It had lost too much. The city of St. Anthony itself was diminished. No longer was it the equal, much less the superior, of Minneapolis. St. Anthony was older and had developed its mills first, but three years after the Eastman Tunnel washed away its industry, St. Anthony was absorbed by Minneapolis, becoming "St. Anthony West."

It would take Eastman a decade to find a solution to his problem of how to get enough waterpower to run Nicollet Island mills. An overland cable did the trick. There would be no more tunneling. The City of Minneapolis had launched a preliminary investigation into Eastman and one of his business partners and cleared them of wrongdoing, both civil and criminal.

George A. Brackett would continue to play a role in industry and in the Minneapolis fire companies. He was later elected mayor of Minneapolis, but for only one term. His crackdown on vice annoyed voters, who had enjoyed their easy access to paid sex, liquor and gambling dens. He lost his bid for reelection.

As for Eastman, he was seen as an angelic philanthropist and a titan of the milling industry. Yes, he was innovative. There's no denying that. And Minneapolis would not have become dominant if Eastman hadn't destroyed the mills of St. Anthony.

THE MILL EXPLOSION

Thunder cracked over the city of Minneapolis at 7:20 p.m. on May 2, 1878. Or at least that's what the residents and workers farther from the falls would have thought for a split-second. But then, for a half-mile around, Minneapolitans' windows shattered. As far away as St. Paul, houses shook. Thousands of Minneapolitans and St. Paulites ran out of their homes. The St. Paulites, fearing that it was an earthquake, made for the St. Anthony Falls. The streets teemed with terrified men, women and children.

Earlier that evening, at 6:00 p.m., the day shift workers began to clock out at the Mill Complex at 700–709 South First and Second Streets, in the Mill District of Minneapolis. Among them were all of the shipping and receiving clerks, maintenance workers and packers for transport, as well as the day shift millers. The night shift consisted of skeleton crews. At the largest mill in the complex, the Washburn "A," fourteen millers would keep the grist ground overnight. They finished clocking in by about 7:12 p.m.

Eight minutes after the shift change, a column of smoke, laced with flames, shot up hundreds of feet in the air over the Washburn "A." That was the first shock. At the second shock, the roof shuddered upward and then fell. As it went, it took out the floors below it, and the walls in turn crashed down. The Diamond and the Humboldt Mills, to the west and the south, respectively, went down as the walls of the Washburn "A" collapsed on them. The "A" went up in flames, cremating the entire night shift. "[S]heets of flame…swept through the district."[60]

The Pettit, Zenith and the Galaxy Mills, farther away on the other side of the canal, burst into flames within minutes. The wooden elevator near the "A" caught on fire and then *became* fire, a tower of kindling. Its iron roof fractured, and a fragment flew two miles away.

Within five minutes, Winslow M. Brackett, now chief engineer of the volunteer firefighters, arrived at the Mill District. The tongues of flame threatened to devour the whole district, but Brackett and his men stood in its way. There was no salvaging the Washburn "A." The firefighters focused their attention on the Washburn "B" mill, which had caught fire immediately after the "A" explosion. Some of Brackett's men had to run off to fight more fires, as the wind carried flaming brands over South Minneapolis and dropped them at will.

By 1:00 a.m. on May 3, the fire was under control. It would be another hour before any of the volunteer firefighters relaxed. Several of their companies were sent home to rest. The flames in the district had not yet died altogether, and the firefighters worked in shifts over the next few days. At last, on the afternoon of Sunday, May 5, their work was done.

The explosion knocked out an entire third of Minneapolis's milling capacity. In addition to the mills themselves, the fire, shocks and falling debris destroyed lumber yards, a railroad roundhouse and a machine shop. Many Mill City residents lost their homes. The Washburn "A," the colossus, the biggest flour mill in the world at that time, had been reduced to a "chaotic pile of huge limestone rocks…interwoven with slivered timbers, shafts and broken machinery from which [poured] forth steam and water."[61] The explosion and its after-effects had leveled the Humboldt and Diamond Mills. Three other mills were skeletons now.

In addition to the fourteen "A" millers, four nearby workers died. There would have been many more fatalities if not for the timing of the explosion. In the Mill District, the shift change from day to night workers occurred at any time between 6:00 p.m. and 8:00 p.m., meaning that the other mills were not fully manned. The bodies were not all found intact, but ten of them could be identified in whole or in fragments. Eight had been burned beyond recognition.

The mills sought to collect on their fire insurance policies. The estimated financial loss tallied more than $1 million. That's in 1878 figures, and it translates to $27 million in today's currency. The insurers didn't cough it up, on the grounds that their policies were for *fire*, not explosions with chemical origins.

Hennepin County empaneled a coroner's jury. On May 20, it convened in the Agricultural College Building of the University of Minnesota. Two scholars from the university appeared before the jury. Louis W. Peck, a physics instructor, and chemistry professor Stephen F. Peckham performed an experiment for the jurors. They held, one after another, nine products of a flour mill over a Bunsen burner. They all caught fire but fizzled in less than five seconds. This was the first of a series of demonstrations. One of them must have been alarming to witness:

An uncovered lighted lamp was placed in a strong wooden box, over which a heavy loose cover was placed. Two men stood on the cover. A small charge of any one of the dusts, except coarse bran [which, prior demonstrations had shown, was less responsive to heat and flame], *blown in by a bellows would take fire from the lamp, explode, lift the cover with the two men, and spread a sheet of flame several feet in all directions.*[62]

Peck explained to the jurors that the dust from flour milling can, in the presence of flame, explode like gunpowder. Peckham added that a ninety-eight-pound flour sack, in combination with four thousand cubic feet of air force, could create an explosion that could blow a 2,500-ton weight one hundred feet high.

What did this mean for the Washburn "A"? Peckham drew the jurors' attention to the structure of the mill. On the east side, six runs of millstones reground middlings. Middlings, commonly called "farina," are a byproduct of flour production. If you've ever eaten Cream of Wheat or Malt-O-Meal, you've had middlings. The meal from these runs emptied onto a single conveyor, which deposited it in an elevator, which in turn brought it upstairs. There, at the conveyor's terminus, a spout with a revolving fan bore off dust

Two days after the explosion of the Washburn "A" Mill. *Hennepin County Library Digital Collections.*

and the hot air from the friction of grinding and swept it along to a small room by the end of the spout for collecting flour dust, called a "dust house," on the side of the mill. All of that was standard operating procedure.

The problem, said Peckham, began at the stones. Either they ran low from insufficient middlings to grind or the grain had been contaminated with a small scrap of metal or gravel. Friction between the surface of the stones and another hard surface generated sparks. Those sparks were carried along the conveyor, up the elevator, through the fan and into the spout. Here, the sparks ignited the dust particles in the dust house. No one had ever cleaned it out. The dust had been accumulating for years, and it was dense and flammable.

That was the first explosion. It shook the building and dislodged more dust. Then came the explosion heard 'round the cities, throwing the roof up and pushing out the walls. The "A" mill flames jumped twenty-five feet over to the Diamond Mill's windows. Having just felt the shock, the Diamond's dust had already loosened when the ignition hit, and the air was thick with flammable material. The Diamond gave the Humboldt the same treatment. Three mills caught fire within a matter of seconds. It had taken observation of how the walls of each mill overlapped one another to prove that they had fallen successively. To those who witnessed the actual event, it had seemed that all three mills simultaneously combusted.

The jurors took more than two weeks in their deliberations. They delivered their verdict on May 22. They commended Peckham's work and unanimously agreed that his interpretation of events was correct. The insurance companies were not convinced that the explosion had been triggered by fire, as opposed to a chemical substance, even though there was no evidence indicating a particular point of origin, which investigators would have found if it been a chemical explosion. However, they were worn down by local pressure. The mills *were* Minneapolis. They had built Minneapolis and were still its economic foundation. All insurance companies that could afford to pay up, paid up, but the mill owners bore the brunt of the loss, to say nothing of the survivors of the eighteen dead.

At least the mill operators had learned. They now kept the mills cleared of dust. Safety standards are written in blood, and "[u]ntil the explosion occurred the latent possibilities of flour dust in this connection were unsuspected."[63] Another good thing to come out of the tragedy was that the volunteer firefighters realized that this was a job for professionals. They had acquitted themselves well and have gone down in history as city heroes. But they had the wisdom to know that Minneapolis needed more than their limited services could offer. In 1879, a year after the mill explosion, the volunteers requested that the municipal government establish a fire department, funded by the city, with paid firefighters. The Minneapolis Fire Department was born, and Winslow Brackett remained the chief engineer. And for years to come, the men of MFD would fear another explosion every time an alarm sounded in the Mill District.

WHEN MILL OWNER CADWALLADER Colden Washburn got the news about losing the entire nightshift, the first thing he did was to travel in the opposite direction from Minneapolis, going southeast to Madison. He wanted to check on the progress of construction on the Washburn Observatory on the University of Wisconsin campus. Only after that did he head up to the Mill City.

In Minneapolis, Washburn's priorities did not include mourning. He immediately got to work rebuilding the mill. It was quite a task. The original so-called Big Mill, the "A," had stood 100 feet by 108 feet and was seven and a half stories high. Before long, it was back up and running. Life went on

The Washburn "A", "B" and "C" Mills, rebuilt after the explosion. *Hennepin County Library Digital Collections.*

for the Washburn "A" and the rest of the Mill City, just as it did not for the victims of the explosion.

On June 2, one month after their deaths, there was a public funeral for the eight men who could not be identified. According to Augustine E. Costello, a witness to the explosion and a historian of the Minneapolis Police and Fire Departments, the Mill District fire was "attended by the greatest loss of life that ever occurred in the Northwest" as of 1890.[64]

Washburn deigned to acknowledge the men his old mill had destroyed, with a stone tablet set into the northeast exterior corner of the new mill:

This mill
was erected in the year 1879
on the site of Washburn Mill A which was
totally destroyed
on the Second day of May, 1878,
by fire and a terrific
explosion occasioned by the rapid combustion of
flour dust. Not
one stone was left upon another,
and every person
engaged in the mill instantly
lost his life.
The following are the names of the faithful
and well tried employees who fell
victims of that awful
calamity, viz:

E.W. BURBANK,   *CYRUS W. EWING,*
E.H. GRUNDMAN,   *HENRY HICKS,*
CHARLES HENNING,   *PATRICK JUDD,*
CHARLES KIMBALL,   *WILLIAM LESLIE,*
FRED A. MERRILL,   *EDWD. E. MERRILL,*
WALTER E. SAVAGE,   *OLE SCHIE,*
AUGUST SMITH,   *CLARK WILBUR.*

"Labor wide as the earth
Has its summit in Heaven."[65]

PART IV

VIOLENCE IN THE MILL CITY

By Means Unknown

Frank McManus was born into a respectable, working-class Southside Boston family. His brother John worked at the Norway rolling mill. His other brother, Michael, was a self-defense instructor. Frank had given his family some cause for worry while he was growing up. He had served time in a reformatory for truancy. Frank straightened himself out by his late teens and learned a trade in scissor-grinding. He worked diligently at two different rolling mills, but the local industry took a brief downturn and he struggled to find work. At the age of twenty or twenty-one, he headed west in search of better opportunities.

Life on the road did not suit Frank, and he se   d two years in prison in Wisconsin. He had given up scissor-grinding in favor of burglary, by which he made his living. From a hardworking tradesman, he transformed into a drunkard and a drifter. He was on his way to nowhere in particular.

Jason F. Spear and his wife, Meribah, were a middle-aged couple from Vermont. In 1882, they were living in Minneapolis at 1016 Fourth Avenue South, on a spot that is now the start of the on-ramp to Southbound Interstate Highway 35 West. Mr. Spear worked as a plumber for Sykes and Andrews, a reputable plumbing company. Mr. and Mrs. Spear had experienced tragedy earlier in their marriage, when their son, Freddie, died in infancy. It took them four years after his death to have another child, Lilla. Five years later, Mrs. Spear gave birth to a second daughter, Mina. They were a happy family, thanks to the joy the parents took in their children, now nine years old and four years old.

Interstate highways didn't exist back then, nor were there any hazards in the neighborhood. On Thursday, April 27, little Mina asked if she could go play in the yard of a family friend, Mrs. Peterson, who lived one block over. Mina knew the way, having been there many times before, and so Mrs. Spear gave her permission to go. Mina skipped off around 2:30 p.m.

Close to 3:00 p.m., Mrs. Peterson stopped over at the Spears' home. Mrs. Spear was confused as to why she hadn't brought Mina with her. Mrs. Peterson replied that she hadn't seen her. Mrs. Spear ran out, frantically searching for Mina. She learned from a pair of little boys who were frequent playmates of her daughter that they had seen Mina after she had left home. In fact, the three children had gone on an outing together. A man had given a nickel to each of the children and then taken them to a store to buy candy. The boys bought themselves sweets, but the man didn't let Mina spend the nickel he had given her. He bought her some candy sticks and asked if she wanted to come with him. The man and Mina left, and that was all that the boys knew about it.

Mrs. Spear knew then that Mina had been kidnapped. Someone telephoned for the police, and a search party got to work in the meantime, bringing the two playmates with them. They didn't have to go far. At Eleventh Street and Fourth Avenue South, one block southwest from the Spears' home and across from the original Central High School (razed in the 1900s), the boys drew their attention to a heavyset, mustachioed white man with a scar on his chin. He was of medium height and wore a slouch hat like a soldier. His blue flannel shirt and coarse-cloth suit were ratty.

Mrs. Spear got in the man's face and demanded Mina's return. The man became belligerent. A neighbor joined in against him, but the man was adamant that he never laid eyes on her. He screamed vulgar abuse at Mina's mother.

AN ENTIRE HOUR HAD elapsed between the time that Mrs. Spear had realized that Mina was missing and the time that Patrolman William Gleason was informed. All that he was told was that a man who looked homeless had taken a little girl from her home on Fourth Avenue South. The moment Gleason got the news, a man named John Mullaney happened to be riding past him in a carriage. Gleason flagged him down, and Mullaney, following his instructions, rushed his horses along Fourth.

Gleason came upon a down-at-the-heels man arguing with two women. As Mullaney's carriage approached, the man looked around and saw Gleason in his uniform. He bolted and Gleason gave chase. Minneapolis had been a city for only twenty-eight years and had a population of only about forty-seven thousand. It was still, in many ways, the Wild West. If Gleason had known the horror that his quarry had inflicted on Mina Spear, he would have shot him in the back. That would have been a more merciful fate than the one that would befall him.

The fleeing suspect only made it two blocks, to Tenth Street and Sixth Avenue, probably about a block and a half northeast of the present-day Minnesota Highway 65 off-ramp. It was there that Gleason seized him. Just fifteen minutes after getting notified of the kidnapping, Gleason had his man. Gleason saw immediately that his instinct had steered him right: the man had blood on his clothes. Gleason compelled the man to get into the carriage with him and brought him to the store that the little boys had told Mrs. Spear about. The store owner immediately recognized him, having seen him earlier that afternoon, buying candy and going off with a little girl. Gleason then took him to the police station, where he conducted an examination of the suspect's person. In addition to a lot of blood on his right hand, as well as his trousers and vest, his underwear was bloody. Gleason charged him with rape and locked him in a holding cell.

In the meantime, a wonderful and terrible thing happened. Near East Eighteenth Street and Three-and-One-Half Avenue South, just east of present-day Stevens Square Park, John Farley, an expressman, found a semiconscious and bloodied Mina Spear. He rushed down the street, bearing the little girl in his arms. It was a half-mile journey from where he had found her to her home on Fourth Avenue South. Mrs. Spear had to call for multiple doctors. Mina was bleeding profusely from hideous lacerations to her genitals. She was barely alive after so much blood loss. In addition to raping her, the assailant had cut her with a knife.

The police arrived at the house to interview Mrs. Spear, but she didn't know much of anything that could help their investigation. They didn't question the traumatized victim, who was still under the doctors' care. Other than the two little witnesses who had come along for candy, the only person who could tell them anything of substance would have to be their suspect.

Dr. Albert A. Ames. *Hennepin County Library Digital Collections.*

There was no need to worry on that front. Detective Michael Hoy was on the case. The forty-eight-year-old Irishman had started out as a stonecutter but soon found his true calling in law enforcement. By 1867, he had become the St. Anthony city marshal. The jail he oversaw, known as "Hoy's little stone jug," was at that time the westernmost jail in the United States.[66] He served in law enforcement until his death in 1895, except for a stint as a captain in the Union army. With all of the experience that Hoy had accumulated by 1882, the suspect didn't stand a chance against him. At first, the man gave up nothing, not even his name.

About three hours after Gleason had hopped into Mullaney's carriage, the bad news had reached the whole city. It was decided then, by general consensus, that the rapist must be lynched. One crowd after another gathered outside the jailhouse. The police guards only allowed journalists and a few others to come in to see the arrested man. After some time, the suspect finally cracked and provided his name: Frank McManus, from Boston. He refused to admit that he had attacked Mina. When questioned about the blood on his hands, trousers and underwear, McManus said that he had gotten into a fight on Wednesday, the night before. The police knew that he was lying because the blood was damp and fresh.

This was a crime so heinous that Mayor Albert Alonzo Ames immediately involved himself in it. His father, Dr. Alfred Elisha Ames, had also stared down the threat of frontier justice. He had been a member of the Barber's Hall committee twenty-six years earlier, after the first two murders in Hennepin County. Dr. A.E. Ames had been a party to the resolution cautioning against lynching the brutal murderers, if caught, of the child Susan Whallen and the young mother Mary Jane Hathaway:

> [W]e have full confidence in the power of the civil authorities to impartially administer the laws, and to legally punish all crimes; [...]we deprecate any attempt on the part of individuals to resort to violence, or to take the execution of the law into their own hands.[67]

Police chief Albert S. Munger joined Hoy and Ames as well. Hoy had worn down McManus by late evening, and he finally confessed to the three of them. He told them that he had first met the children by a peanut stand. After giving Mina candy, he brought her to a woodyard, and there he attacked her. He did not tell them what had possessed him to do such a vicious thing. Hoy had McManus's bloodied pants taken for evidence.

Four years earlier, Munger had told the city that the number of drifters wandering through Minneapolis was rising and that, in 1877, his men had identified more than four hundred such persons. Most of them, he said, were just looking for work, but a solid one-third were predators searching for fresh prey. McManus was exactly the sort of man he had in mind. Munger had made it a mission of his police department to persecute the homeless. Thanks in part to his efforts and influence, by the late 1880s, after this story takes place, being suspected of homelessness by the police could yield a thirty- to sixty-day stint in the workhouse. The police department, under both Munger and his successors, waged a war not on poverty, but on the poor.

Munger would have been the last person alive to care for McManus's safety, but his love of the law exceeded his antipathy toward the homeless. He feared the ominous crowds and the calls for lynching—at least, that's the official narrative. At any rate, he decided, at 10:35 p.m., to move McManus out of his lockup to the Hennepin County Jail, on the site of the present-day U.S. Bank Stadium.

That meant turning him over to Sheriff James Mace Eustis, a fifty-five-year old, Maine-born businessman. Eustis was a born entrepreneur, and he had been barely out of boyhood when he opened his market stall at the storied Faneuil Hall in Boston. Among his many accomplishments since his arrival in Minneapolis, he had led the project to build the Nicollet House hotel in 1858, supplied all the Minnesota soldiers' rations in the Civil War and built an entire block of Hennepin Avenue. He was a pillar of society and a city father. In 1880, he ran for Hennepin County sheriff. Although Eustis ran as a Democrat, he was so good natured and well liked that he won votes from Minneapolitans of all political parties.

On the night of April 27, Eustis knew that a mob would come to make an attempt on McManus's life. County sheriff was a day job,

J. Mace Eustis. *Hennepin County Library Digital Collections.*

but he decided to work the night shift this time. The buck would stop with him. McManus was placed in a cell upstairs, in the third tier of the county jail.

Come midnight, the crowds were moving with more purpose, and the collective mob of masked men seemed to have a mind of its own. A thirst for blood drew them to the jail, where they arrived at 1:00 a.m. and demanded that Eustis let them in. Eustis told them they couldn't come in, but they ignored him. Several of the men, working together, slammed their shoulders into the door and busted it open. They told Eustis, "We want that man."

"You can't have him," he replied.[68] Eustis stood firm, verbally and physically. When he attempted to block the mob, four or five men wrestled the late-middle-aged sheriff down into a dark corner and restrained him. They demanded the jail keys and that Eustis tell them where McManus was. He refused. A locked, iron door barred the mob's access to the main corridor of the jail cells.

It was 1:20 a.m. when the men first took their sledgehammers to the door. They alternated with each other, one group standing guard in case anyone came to stop them while the other group hammered. It took them one hundred minutes, until 3:00 a.m., to breach the door. A collective murmur of satisfaction rippled through the crowd. They proceeded to smash through the cells on the first floor. The prisoners probably feared for their lives, and they told them where to find McManus: upstairs.

There were two men in the third-tier cell. One of them told the mob that the other had come in a few hours earlier. The latter said that he was not the man they were looking for and gave his name as Tim Crowley. To make sure that they had the right man, a contingent went to the jail office and consulted the records. Whenever a person was jailed, their name and physical description was logged in a book. Although there was no Crowley in the book, the description of the rapist's face and clothing pointed the finger at the man in the cell. Not all of the men were persuaded. Rather than harm the wrong person, the mob leaders decided to bring the man who called himself Crowley to the Spear home. If Mrs. Spear did not recognize him, they planned to bring him back to the jail. If she *did* recognize him…

Fifteen minutes with a sledgehammer yielded an open cell door and the sought-after prisoner. He betrayed no emotion as they pulled him from the cell. His cellmate exclaimed, "I want my pants. Those are my pants. He didn't have any on when he came here."

The mob handcuffed the man who was now their prisoner. It was 3:20 a.m. when they left the jailhouse. They arrived at Mina's neighborhood around 3:40 a.m. They did not concern themselves with guilt or innocence but instead with identification. They woke up the women who had been in the search party, or who at least had witnessed the confrontation between the suspect and Mrs. Spear that afternoon. All of them verified that this was the man who had argued with Mrs. Spear. Finally, they brought him into the Spear house, disturbing Mrs. Spear at 4:00 a.m. Mrs. Spear knew the man instantly. "That's the man; take him away, take him away. Oh! those eyes, I shall never forget them!"

"It's a mistake," he said.[69]

Mrs. Spear's positive identification had sealed his fate. According to one source, Mina also was awake and identified him as the rapist.[70] The mob hauled McManus off in search of a tree. They found what they were looking for, on the lot at Grant and Fourth Avenue South, across from Central High. One man among the mob climbed the tree, eager to be the one to string the rope. They didn't know it then, but McManus had been sitting under that tree when he called the three children over to him.

The men shouted questions at McManus. He denied everything, and they shouted that he lied and told him, "We're going to make a terrible example of you."[71] He maintained his innocence and repeated that he was Tim Crowley, not Frank McManus. He then spoke quietly to a few of the leaders who stood nearby. McManus also stated, loudly enough to be heard by more of them, what he might have hoped would be a mitigating circumstance: he had been drunk when he attacked Mina. It wasn't mitigating to the mob. They tied McManus's hands behind his back and set the noose around his neck. McManus clenched his fists, perhaps to steel himself for the ordeal to come or as an involuntary response. The men tugged the rope over a tree limb, working together to yank him high and tie the rope to the tree trunk.

> Creak went the rope over the tree limb, and McManus swung clear of the ground. Two more pulls and he was whirling round and round in the air. The end of the rope was fastened to the trunk of the tree, and at precisely four o'clock, a sigh of relief went up from the crowd. Some started away, but others remained to watch him die. Five minutes later, there was a convulsive twitching of the legs and all was over.[72]

About twelve and a half hours after the police had been informed of Mina's kidnapping, Frank McManus was dead.

On an unofficial level, the police knew about the lynching. Sergeant Swan S. Walton, Minneapolis PD, a forty-two-year-old Swede, was fascinated by the hanging. About an hour after after McManus's death, he went with his friend William O'Brien to the lot to see the dangling corpse. O'Brien, a young Irish immigrant, was working as a watchman at the Milwaukee Depot, which still stands at 201 Third Avenue South, about two blocks southwest of the Highway 65/Third Avenue Bridge. On his way to the depot after gawking at the corpse, O'Brien had an idea.

DAWN CAME. IN THE streets, those Minneapolitans who had not yet heard about the lynching now learned of it. By 7:00 a.m. more than a thousand men, women and children had gathered around the tree, which was now being guarded by the police. Patrolman Lindell S. Caswell recognized the hanged man as McManus, whom he had seen at the police station the day before. Photographers took pictures. Policemen stood guard at the scene until Coroner A.C. Fairbairn's arrival. Fairbairn arrived at the lot around 7:40 a.m. and had the corpse brought down. McManus's slouch hat fell on the ground, and souvenir hunters dove for it. Their competition for the hat tore it to pieces, which the scavengers brought home with them. The body was loaded into a wagon and taken down Fourth Avenue South, past the Spears' home, and on to N.F. Warner's undertaking parlor. In the absence of a body or, after the coroner's departure, a police guard, the crowd swarmed the tree. A lucky few made off with bits of the rope. Over the next few days, the bark of the tree was stripped for keepsakes.

Word got around that William O'Brien had picked up a section of the rope that was used to hang McManus. He was selling off pieces of it, and eager Minneapolitans flooded the Milwaukee Depot in the hopes of purchasing a ghoulish souvenir. O'Brien enjoyed a small amount of fame and fortune. He dined and smoked on other men's dimes. In truth, he had snuck a nine-foot length of rope from the baggage room, hidden it and then "confided" to a few coworkers that he had gotten it from the oak tree. The hoax went undiscovered for years.

Fairbairn, unlike most coroners, especially of his day, had a medical degree. However, he did not perform the postmortem examination. This was no more the coroner's role than it was the mayor's, who, incidentally, also had a medical degree. The honor fell to Dr. A.R. Brackett, who taught anatomy at the Minnesota College Hospital, and his fellow physician, R.J. Hill, who served for a long time as head of the Hennepin Medical Society. The pair were vastly overqualified to perform this task. The Central students across the street from the hanging could as easily have determined the cause of death.

Fairbairn held the farce of a coroner's inquest on Saturday, April 29, in Warner's parlor. All of the police officers who had interacted with McManus on Thursday testified about their encounters with him, as did Mayor Ames. An acquaintance of McManus's from Boston conclusively identified the body as belonging to him. Brackett and Hill presented their conclusion that McManus had died from hanging. Eustis alone mentioned the mob, as he told of its invasion into his jail and its members' assault on him:

> [I] *did not recognize any of them; they were disguised; I saw hammers and timbers in the jail next morning, which I suppose they used to break down the doors; the man whose body I have seen is the man who was taken away; they took him away about 4 o'clock.*[73]

Mina was still at death's door. Her doctors weren't sure that she would make it. This almost certainly influenced the jury to return the following verdict: "He came to his death by strangulation, by means unknown to the jury."[74]

After that, McManus's body was made available for public viewing. In those days, people did not request that their bodies be donated to medical schools. It was a fate typically reserved for recipients of the death penalty. An exception was made for McManus. The city government decided that it was "best not to desecrate God's acre with its unholy presence."[75]

His body was donated to Brackett's institution for teaching purposes, without giving his family back in Boston a chance to bury him. They reacted with shock and disbelief to the news of Frank's crime, as nothing in his history could have led them to predict such a terrible act. One of his brothers had previously had a coworker named Jim Crowley, from whom Frank McManus had probably drawn inspiration for his alias. There was no question that the lynched man, the rapist of a four-year-old, was Frank. His sisters wanted desperately to know what he had said so quietly to the leaders of the lynch mob. They would never know. Who the leaders were and what they heard has never been divulged to the public. To this day, we do not know the identity of a single member of that mob.

Reporters had entered the county jail with the mob, ducking out every hour or so to give their editors live updates. They surely knew who the members of the masked mob were. Some of them may have been full-fledged members of it, and others may have feared those who were and kept their secret. Newspapers near and far sympathized with the mob. The

Minneapolis Evening Journal declared that "[t]here was a higher law that made his instant death necessary, and we thank God that there were men in Minneapolis brave and manly enough to execute it promptly."[76]

The *Winona Republican* sinisterly remarked, "[Minneapolis] understands to a nicety the art of adjusting hempen neck-ties where they belong."[77]

The *Journal* of Madison, Wisconsin, was ultimately in agreement with the mob, without being nearly so gleeful or congratulatory as other papers. The journalist argued that the murder of McManus "is a thing to be regretted by every lover of good order," yet his crime was so horrifying that "the public sentiment is inclined rather to sustain than censure the mob which dealt out summary punishment so richly deserved by the culprit."[78]

In case of Mina's survival, McManus would have been charged with rape, which is not a capital offense. The fact that McManus would face no harsher legal sentence than prison only amplified support for his killers. As the *Minneapolis Tribune* put it, "The punishment provided by law…fails to even approach the measure of legal expiation demanded by the universal popular heart." So "universal" was this "heart," said the *Tribune*, that "[t]he hanging of McManus with the omission of the usual legal formalities is not condemned by this community, nor, so far as known, by any person residing in this community." The reason for this was that "[o]bviously no injustice was done to the criminal."[79]

"[W]ell-deserved vengeance," said the *Chicago Tribune*.[80]

The *St. Paul Pioneer Press* expressed a similar sentiment: "The punishment visited upon him was not too severe—no punishment can be imagined too severe for [such] a crime.…[McManus] forfeit[ed] every claim upon human tolerance or mercy." A few sentences later, there appeared the oxymoronic claim that the lynching "was inspired by…the righteous wrath that arms the ministers of the law with power to punish and erects a bulwark against the evil impulses of the depraved."[81] In other words, if men like the April 27 mob *didn't* go around murdering criminals, then the authority of the law would be diminished. Sheriff Eustis would probably beg to differ.

By modern standards, the local authorities did not come out of this looking good, but things were different back then and it didn't hurt their careers. Although Mayor Ames would lose the next election (for reasons related to his shameless corruption, not because of the public lynching in his city), he would make a comeback. In twenty years' time, he would rule the Minneapolis underworld. Eustis, who fought against a mob for the sake of legal justice, did not serve another term as sheriff. His civic-mindedness did not desert him, however. He never accumulated much wealth, in spite of his business acumen, because he put the money he earned from his real estate ventures back into the city. He helped build Minneapolis, in every sense of the word.

There was good news in store for the Spear family. A benefit fund raised quite a bit of money for Mina's care. Mr. and Mrs. Spear feared for a few days that they would bury their daughter, but she survived. Mina's physicians worked miracles, and she was also lucky. Not only did she live to middle age, outliving her mother, but she also recovered so completely from her injuries that, in adulthood, she bore a child, Edward.

THE FAMILY THAT SLAYS TOGETHER

Flames sprang from the six-story windows of the Big Boston Minneapolis, a gigantic candle on a hot summer night. The Big Boston was a multistate chain of retail clothing stores. The Minneapolis location had its own building in the commercial block at Washington Avenue South and Second Avenue South. The upper floors held a large quantity of excelsior, wood shavings used in packaging for shipment. This kindling led the fire straight to the roof. The timbers collapsed, knocking over the top of the west wall, which crashed down onto the next building. Every fire engine in the city was brought to the rescue. The firefighters had controlled the spread by about midnight, in time to save the lower two stories of both buildings, but the financial damages amounted to anywhere between $500,000 to $750,000 (about $14 million to $21 million today).

EARLIER THAT EVENING, ON July 26, 1887, Mrs. Minnie Barrett had been chatting with some friends on the porch of her home at 2830 First Avenue South. Her husband, Henry "Reddy" Barrett, left with two of his brothers, Tim and Pete, who had recently come to town. Mrs. Barrett and her guests settled down for the night, around 11:00 p.m. She woke up sometime later to the sound of Reddy coming upstairs. Her husband and brothers-in-law went out again the next evening.

IN THE EARLY HOURS of July 28, Streetcar no. 132 on the Cedar Avenue line was delayed. The destruction from the fire on the twenty-sixth, and the

Above: Thomas Tollefson. *Library of Congress: Chronicling America.*

Right: Illustration of the Tollefson murder (inset). *Library of Congress: Chronicling America.*

resulting repairs, had affected traffic, holding up several lines. At one o'clock in the morning, the driver, Thomas Tollefson, made it to the turntable near Layman's Cemetery at 2945 Cedar Avenue South, now the Pioneers and Soldiers Memorial Cemetery. He was never seen alive again.

Around two o'clock in the morning, another driver found Tollefson. He lay dead on the front platform of the streetcar, shot in the thigh and the head. The fare box, containing twenty dollars, had been stolen.

FIVE DAYS LATER, ON August 2, a Richfield farmer named Lewis Rheil approached a policeman. Unfortunately, the policeman he chose was no paragon of conscientiousness: Lieutenant Swan S. Walton, who, five years earlier, had gone with his friend to view McManus's strung-up corpse. Rheil told Walton that he had been threshing wheat close to Minnehaha when he overheard three men plotting a robbery. Walton later testified at the murder trial, "I took no stock in what he told me, and to get rid of him I told him to get some whisk[e]y and get them drunk. I did not make any note of it."[82]

The police initially offered a $200 reward for information leading to the conviction of Tollefson's killer. Then Mayor Ames chipped in $1,000, and contributions rolled in from Tollefson's coworkers and employer, the Minneapolis Street Railway Company. No one came forward. Tollefson's wife buried him without knowing who had killed her husband.

———

In the late spring of that year, a month or so before Tollefson's murder, a spate of robberies broke out in South Minneapolis—*nightly* robberies. Homes were frequently burgled as well. The Minneapolis Police Department had no definite theories and no leads. The crimes were escalating. Then, the worst happened: a wealthy tourist at Minnehaha was robbed as well.

Today, Minnehaha Regional Park is a peaceful oasis from the city, despite Highway 55 coursing under Longfellow Park to the immediate southwest and Ford Parkway crossing the Mississippi River to cut through its northern tip. Visitors can play golf, settle down to eat in a picnic area or follow one of the many nature trails to the Minnehaha Falls. The Minnesota Veterans Home couldn't have found a more scenic spot with such easy access to the amenities of urban living. In the 1880s, the park was a summer resort that attracted tourists from all over the country.

One night, a masked, armed robber shot through the window of the telegraph operator at Minnehaha Falls. The operator gave the man everything he asked for. The next day, a guest at the resort had a gun pulled on her. The gunman demanded everything of value that she wore or carried. She handed over $350 in cash, about $11,500 today, as well as her diamond necklace and her gold watch and chain. Finally, the police took action. The city couldn't afford to lose that lucrative tourist traffic.

Three policemen visited Minnehaha, where they found Timothy "Tim" Barrett lounging in the sun. He leaped up and tried to draw his revolver, but the policemen trained their Smith & Wessons on him. He put up his

Minnehaha Falls and footbridge. *Hennepin County Library Digital Collections.*

hands in surrender. While disarming him, the policemen found a knife and some other weapons. Tim never did tell them where he had hidden the stolen goods and cash. His dad, John Barrett, provided a sizable bond for his release from Hennepin County Jail.

John Barrett had been a wealthy farmer in Iowa until he and his wife divorced. Mrs. Barrett retained custody of seven of their eight children. She moved to South Omaha and bought a house. John had custody of Reddy. The two of them went to California, then to Omaha and then Sioux City. None of Barrett's business ventures panned out. In Sioux City, his saloon lasted for a while, but it must not have been enough. In the autumn of 1882, in Minneapolis, he set up an illegal saloon at 2830 First Avenue South, in what is now southeast Whittier. John and Reddy were in and out of the Hennepin County Jail for selling liquor without a license. Their rowdy saloon was dubbed the "Hub of Hell," and policemen would still flinch at the memory of it years after it was shut down. Still, it was a living, and one that allowed twenty-year-old Reddy to marry Minnie, who came from a good Northfield family.

The site of the "Hub of Hell" saloon (2830 First Avenue S), not as exciting as it used to be. *Author's collection.*

The entire Barrett family was a little sketchy, with Mrs. Barrett and her daughters back in Omaha under suspicion of counterfeiting and committing arson for insurance fraud. The authorities were positive that Reddy, Tim and Pete had been involved in, if not responsible for, the Big Boston fire. One of the other Barrett children, Jack, died from a gunshot wound he'd gotten in a barroom brawl. Seventeen-year-old Pete was capable of working hard and could have made a good living for himself as a laborer, but he spent too much of his time with twenty-three-year-old Tim. Between them, they had served time in prisons in Nebraska and Iowa for larceny and highway robbery. Out of prison, they were back at it and were caught with stolen goods in January 1887. They left their mother's home and came to Minneapolis. They lived with their father and Reddy, but they did not make their living at the saloon or at any other place of business. For all of John's failings as a father, he may have been the better parent, and Reddy blamed Mrs. Barrett for his brothers' terrible outcomes.

Two weeks after John bailed Tim out of jail, Thomas Tollefson was dead.

Two weeks after that, Reddy once again found himself in the Hennepin County Jail for illegal liquor sales. The jailer knew him well at that point and noticed that the young man was out of spirits, pacing with his head hung low. That wasn't like him at all.

"Reddy," said the jailer, "what is the matter with you? Why don't you cheer up?"

"Well," said Reddy, "it is all well enough for you to be merry, but if you had on your mind what I have on mine, you would feel down-hearted too."

The jailer got the sense that Reddy had something of a criminal nature that he wanted to get off his chest. He was chatting with Reddy the next day when the prisoner asked him, "What could you do for a man that could tell you all about the Tollefson murder?"

"We could do a great deal," said the jailer.

"Well then," said Reddy, "send for the county attorney."[83]

The next day, Assistant Hennepin County Attorney Robert Jamison arrived at the jail with Inspector Hoy, and Reddy told them a story. On the evening of July 27, 1887, he said, the three brothers had gone out of the house. Although they had no obvious plan for mischief, they were prepared for it, as Tim and Pete were armed with revolvers. On the way home, Tim decided that they should rob a streetcar driver, who would have cash on hand. They came up to Tollefson while he was on the turntable and tried to rob him of the fare box at gunpoint. Tollefson refused to give it to them. Pete shot at him and then ran with Henry toward the cemetery. Henry heard another shot, and then Tim came up to them, carrying the cash box. "I killed him, shot him through the head."[84]

That night, Detective Hoy took Reddy to 2830 First Avenue South. They ripped out the flooring and dug two feet down in the dirt, where they uncovered the streetcar checks that the brothers had found in the fare box and hidden away. Reddy told the police that he and Tim had destroyed the fare box with an axe and threw the pieces into Rice Lake in Wisconsin.

Lieutenant Daniel A. Day led the expedition. He had been in Minneapolis for a long time. He was an older man, in his early fifties. He had moved to the Mill City more than three decades earlier and had been a policeman for eighteen years. After all that time, he was well acquainted

County Attorney Jamison. *Library of Congress: Chronicling America.*

with the environs for many, *many* miles around. He had been up to Rice Lake before, about one hundred miles northeast of Minneapolis. Owing to his familiarity with the locale, he was the one who brought Reddy, Chief Inspector of Detectives James W. Hankinson and Irish-born Lieutenant Thomas Coskran to Rice Lake. Reddy told them that he and Tim had tossed the evidence near a pole in the water.

The men split into two boats. After three hours, they had nearly crossed the lake when they finally located the pole. They may have thought that it would be an easy task to drag the lake from that point because Rice Lake was only six feet deep. They got to work with their wood-and-wire scoops. Over the course of an hour and a half, the policemen scooped up mud and weeds…but no tin scraps of a fare box. The policemen were growing frustrated. The sun was hot on the outside of their heads, and their heads were hot on the inside from frustration. Day told Reddy that the problem was *not* the scoops, which were perfectly adequate, but that the scraps just weren't there. Hankinson and Coskran cursed at Reddy in their irritation.

Even before Reddy's confession, Hankinson had suspected Tim of the Tollefson murder and had him in custody. Hankinson had no evidence for this—only a hunch. The police had not released to the public the reason for the arrest because they hadn't wanted any of his accomplices to go underground. Now that Reddy had implicated Pete, they knew to focus on him. His whereabouts were unknown. The city offered a large reward for information, and the police ultimately heard that Pete had left town. A few days later, they learned of his current city of residence and shortly thereafter tracked him down in South Omaha. There, he was doing honest, hard work, grading a railroad track. He was arrested and brought back to Minneapolis.

When Pete was hauled in, Jamison instructed the detectives to bring him to an office room. It must have been a very large, or else a very crowded, office room: Jamison, Hankinson, Hoy and Detective James Howard were present, along with a stenographer, some patrolmen and a police commissioner. Pete asked them why he had been hauled off to Minneapolis. The officials led him to believe that a gang of streetcar drivers were out for his blood to avenge the murder of Tollefson. One of the two suspects, either Pete or Tim, had told the interrogators that their lawyer had told them not to answer questions from the police and to tell them to go to hell. Tim and Pete ended up telling a story of their own: They said that Reddy was the gunman.

Furious citizens discussed among themselves whether they should lynch the brothers but decided against it, trusting the law this time.

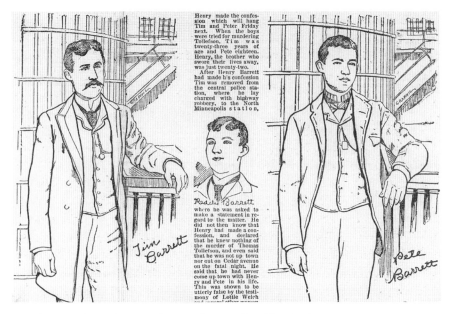

Henry made the confession which will hang Tim and Peter Friday next. When the boys were tried for murdering Tollefson, Tim was twenty-three years of age and Pete eighteen. Henry, the brother who swore their lives away, was just twenty-two.

After Henry Barrett had made his confession Tim was removed from the central police station, where he lay charged with highway robbery, to the North Minneapolis station,

Reddy Barrett

where he was asked to make a statement in regard to the matter. He did not then know that Henry had made a confession, and declared that he knew nothing of the murder of Thomas Tollefson, and even said that he was not up town nor out on Cedar avenue on the fatal night. He said that he had never come up town with Henry and Pete in his life. This was shown to be utterly false by the testimony of Lottie Welch

Tim, Pete and Reddy Barrett. *Library of Congress: Chronicling America.*

Reddy wasn't under arrest, but he was under police surveillance and feared for his own life—not at the hands of a mob, but at the hand of his own brother, Frank. Frank had said that he would kill Reddy on sight for snitching on Tim and Pete. Reddy could never have kept that secret for long. Managing an illegal saloon was one thing. Homicide was something else.

WHILE TIM WAS VISIBLY frightened by the charges against him when they were read in court, Pete was the true object of pity. When the brothers appeared in court post-arraignment, a reporter remarked that Pete "is little else but a boy.…[H]e looked little like a murderer. He is a lad of medium height, somewhat slim." The teenage defendant was shabbily dressed. He wore a hickory shirt, which he tried to conceal by buttoning his coat up to his chin. His checked trousers were too short and had a patched hole in the left knee, and his shoes had multiple holes. Pete's anxiety was written all over his "smooth-shaven, small face[,] [which] looked white in contrast with his reddish hair. His small, narrow eyes roved from one face to another, as though seeking sympathy among the crowd." It showed, also, in his "red and ch[a]pped hands, [in which] he kept twisting a small fur cap, and occasionally laid it down, only to draw from his pocket a dirty blue silk handkerchief, and wipe his face with it."

W.H. Donahue, one of the brothers' attorneys, pointed at the younger boy and said to Assistant City Attorney Rand, "There is the terrible desperado we have been reading so much about of late. Dangerous looking man, is he not?" Pete looked up and smiled at his attorney's sarcasm before looking down again.

"Humph!" said Rand. "I would like to meet about seventeen men like that on a cold night; it would be any amount of fun."[85]

Pete and Tim were tried separately, and their trials were sensational. Donahue was a well-respected attorney, and his partner, William Wallace Erwin, was a heroic defense attorney. Erwin, known as the "Tall Pine of the Northwest" for his towering personality as well as his height, was the best in the business. If he and Donahue couldn't get a "not guilty" verdict, then no one could. They took the defendants' claim that Reddy was the killer and ran with it. The correspondent for the *St. Paul Globe* was just one audience member among many who took this argument at face value when Tim testified to it:

> *Timothy does not make a very good witness and it was apparent to any one before he had been on the stand five minutes, that he was little more than a chump compared with Henry, and that he was the last man in the world to plan an enterprise or to act as a leader. One of the attorneys present said that it appeared to him as the height of folly to think for a moment of such a man being the principal in any kind of an affair in which as smart and cunning a person as Henry Barrett was an accomplice.*[86]

The reporter didn't realize that a chump makes his money by armed robbery, and an intelligent person washes his hands of said chump at the first opportunity.

Tim had given his testimony on December 27, 1887. Excitement built over the next week, as Pete testified against Reddy, who was notably not charged along with his co-conspirators, and a sister testified that Tim was, in modern terms, mentally ill and intellectually disabled. She may have been telling the truth. He was clearly not a person who made good choices. For unrelated reasons, Reddy threatened a journalist with bodily harm. For all these excitements at the outset, by the end of February, the press was growing bored. The Barrett defense team was up against not only Rand but also his boss, County Attorney Frank F. Davis. Davis is one of the most

F.F. Davis. *Library of Congress: Chronicling America.*

Sheriff Ege. *Library of Congress: Chronicling America.*

famous prosecutors in the history of Hennepin County, and his reputation was well earned. He was rigorous, subtle, sometimes sly and thorough almost to the point of compulsiveness. Every scrap of the extensive physical evidence that the police had eventually gathered in the Barrett case and every word of testimonial evidence (aside from the defendants') pointed to Tim and Pete as the gunmen. Davis and Donahue slowly, carefully, made mincemeat of the defense. The *St. Paul Daily Globe*'s sullen headline perfectly encapsulated the disappointment of the press: "A FIGHT FOR LIFE. The Trial of Barrett Drags Its Weary Length Along at Minneapolis."[87] Tim was convicted of murder.

Pete, who hadn't fired the kill shot, hoped for acquittal on the murder charge, arguing that he had only meant to commit robbery. As the evidence against the two of them was so damning, this was ultimately the only point of interest. Davis was determined to nail him on the murder charge and fought hard for it. The *Globe* remarked admiringly, "HE FLIES HIGH, Does County Attorney Davis in His Address."[88] Pete was convicted of murder. He collapsed in his chair when the verdict was read in court. The brothers were sentenced to death.

Governor McGill issued warrants for execution for the day of July 13, 1888. Pete held out hope for a commutation until about half-past nine o'clock in the morning, a few hours before his execution. Pete insisted, to the last, that he had not intended homicide. Sheriff James H. Ege had sent out 150 invitations to the hanging. More people wanted to attend, but the jail yard where the execution would take place could only hold so many. Outside the yard, 5,000 spectators without invitations got a view of the event.

At eleven o'clock on the dot, an officer opened the door to the cells. Father James McGollick led a procession of six men, including the prisoners. He recited the litany for the dying with them. Tim radiated dread, his face sickly. Pete kept it together, but he still looked pale. A sheriff's deputy and a priest escorted each young man to his death.

The Barrett double-scaffold. *Library of Congress: Chronicling America.*

There were two of everything. Two brothers. Two outfits that Sheriff Ege had picked out for them, identical down to the underwear. There were two gallows that Sheriff Ege had set up, right next to each other. As the two prisoners, with their entourage, stepped onto the scaffold, a ray of light shone through a grated window and rested on the heads of the condemned pair. Their time had come and they knew it. Tim knelt, and a priest held a crucifix toward him as McGollick continued the litany. In a loud, mechanical voice, Tim said, "Have mercy on me. Have mercy on me."

The nooses adjusted, the caps pulled down, Pete asked that the jailer shift him toward the front of the scaffold, not wanting his body to hit it as he dropped. Then Ege put his hand on the lever.

"Have mercy on us," the brothers intoned. "Have mercy on us." The mob outside the yard cheered and shouted.

Pete cried out, "God have mercy." Ege pulled the lever, and they dropped.

Tim moved his hands a little for a few seconds. Pete's body "swung around for a few moments and quivered like an aspen."[89] Both of them took about fourteen minutes to die. Ege must have enjoyed that symmetry.

Ege had not allowed women to attend the hanging. Pete's girlfriend, Addie Body, and Mrs. Barrett were both excluded, to their grief. Ege had treated the deaths of their loved ones as public entertainment, setting them up for a visual spectacle. And he had refused those two women the right to be there with the brothers in person. Pete was only eighteen years old when he died.

THE STREETCAR STRIKE

Washington [A]venue looked desolate without the [street]cars, which always have seemed a permanent feature of the landscape.[90]

—*Eva McDonald*

Thomas Lowry. *Hennepin County Library Digital Collections.*

Thomas Lowry, a young Illinoisan attorney, showed up in Minneapolis in 1867 with hardly any resources to his name. Within four years, he made partner at a law firm, then married and got into real estate, where the real money was—and still is—in Minneapolis. Ten years later, he had handled, through sales and purchases, an entire one-third of the land that Minneapolis now covers. The present-day Lowry Hill neighborhood, in southwest Minneapolis, was the site of his home. The legacy of collective wealth reverberates to this day. Lowry Hill is among the most expensive neighborhoods in the city and rich in cultural institutions, most significantly the Basilica of Saint Mary and the Walker Art Center.

Lowry realized that he could buy up the outlying prairie lands and sell them at prices closer to the price of urban real estate, but only if potential residents could be assured of easy access to the city proper. With a partner, he built up and improved the Minneapolis Street Railway Company (MSRC). In 1878, at the age of thirty-five, Thomas Lowry became president of the MSRC. He would hold this position until his death in 1909.

Lowry's streetcars gave Minneapolis a defining feature now considered a downside: urban sprawl. He saw instant success in luring prospective homebuyers to far-flung residences. The city grew along with the streetcar lines, as did the suburbs.

ON THE MORNING OF Thursday, April 11, 1889, day shift workers from the suburbs and the outskirts of Minneapolis hopped aboard the streetcar as they always did. They were bound for the factories and workshops where they labored. By the time they had their lunch break, the flow of streetcars had slowed. By 4:00 p.m., it had ceased. As their shifts wrapped up, the workers came outside. Streetcar drivers and conductors stood among the crowd, watching their would-be passengers hold out hope for a car that would never come. Some of the downtown workers waited thirty minutes for a streetcar, while others waited longer than that. They didn't want to walk home after a full day's work, but they didn't have a choice. It was an important lesson about how much they had come to rely on the streetcars.

That morning, streetcar employees had arrived at the carbarns, which are like garages for streetcars and buses. There they found a posted notice from their employer:

> *To employes of the Minneapolis Street Railway Company:*
> *Owing to shrinkage in receipts and increased outlay, we are compelled to reduce expenses in all departments.*
> *From and after April 14 the following will be the scale of wages:*
> *Conductors and drivers on street cars, 15 cents per hour…*
> *Conductors on motor line, 17 cents per hour…*

The notice was dated for April 10, but it had been snuck into the carbarns overnight.[91] It practically amounted to a breach of contract. Eleven months earlier, on May 13, 1888, the Street Railway Employees Protective Union had struck against the MSRC. The strike was a resounding success, resulting in an agreement with the company, effective for twelve months. The conditions of the agreement were very favorable to the employees. It guaranteed them pay raises after three months, up to seven days' vacation time after six months on the job and unlimited sick leave. The final, fifteenth provision was the most important: "This agreement shall be binding on the company and on the employes [sic] for one year from date."[92] The notice that the streetcar workers found pinned up in the carbarns informed them of pay cuts, in violation of the fifteenth provision. Streetcar drivers and conductors took the most insulting hit, with their new wages lower than the previous starting wage.

Not only had Lowry violated the agreement of May 1888 by unilaterally cutting pay, but he had also been taking steps to break up the union. Starting in November, the MSRC had been firing workers at random and hiring new workers who had to sign an agreement as a condition of employment. The workers referred to this as the "iron-clad." It was a pledge that "I will not, while in [the] employ [of the MSRC], join or belong to any labor organization. A violation of this agreement will be sufficient cause for my discharge."[93]

As soon as they saw the April 11 notice of 15 percent pay cuts, members of the union got on the streetcars. They rode all over the city, bringing it to the attention of all of their coworkers. Drivers and conductors abandoned their cars right there on the line or brought them back to the carbarns. To coincide with the carbarn notices, Lowry printed a statement in the morning papers, laying out his company's finances. Creative bookkeeping gave a surface impression that the company was suffering and couldn't continue to pay its workers at the agreed-upon rates. One journalist remarked, "Some people think it is a true statement. Others regard it as a joke."[94]

MSRC employees and labor advocates knew that it was nonsense that Lowry needed to make cuts. His company was believed to be worth more than $5 million, which is about $148 million today. Lowry didn't need to get extra cash by snatching it away from his employees. In truth, he was adapting the lines to run on electric cables. He wouldn't need as many conductors as were currently on the payroll. His company wouldn't suffer at all if some of them quit.

THERE IMMEDIATELY EMERGED A class of men who saw a business opportunity: the drivers of all sorts of vehicles, now offering passenger transport to pick up the streetcars' slack. Adventure-seekers took advantage as well, flooding city hall with the aim of being appointed special policemen. A contingent of army veterans marched to the MSRC HQ. There they "enrolled themselves as special protectors of the public peace."[95]

An earnest, bright-eyed young woman approached them and addressed one of the new "special protectors." She asked him, "Do you fear any disturbance because the employes [sic] of the street railway have quit work?"

The man replied, "In time of peace prepare for war[.] It is hard to tell what those strikers may do, and we will be prepared for them."[96]

Shortly after that, at Minneapolis PD HQ, the same young woman ran into some MSRC employees. They were among the applicants for an appointment as special policemen. She asked them, "Why do you apply for those places?

"We are sure that the striking employes [sic] will offer no resistance to law, but outsiders may make some mischievous attempt to injure property, and we are willing to do anything in our power to preserve order," one of the men answered. She never did learn whether any of them managed to secure an appointment.

The woman was Eva McDonald, a twenty-three-year-old, Maine-born labor journalist with the *St. Paul Daily Globe*, writing under the pseudonym

"Eva Gay." She had once inspired a strike at a Minneapolis garment factory: she had described the poor working conditions in her news articles, and seeing their plight in print emboldened the abused workers to assert their rights. For her passionate, articulate advocacy for the rights of workers, the Farmers' Alliance had elected her as a state lecturer. But right now, she was following the streetcar strike every step of the way.

THAT EVENING, THE LABOR Temple on Fourth Street Southeast was packed. Streetcar workers aired their grievances about the job. Even with the provisions in the 1888 agreement in place, their work was hard. They worked odd hours, with unpredictable sleep schedules and meal times. And those guaranteed wages still weren't enough to comfortably support a family. There wasn't any room in their household budgets for a pay cut. Although the MSRC hadn't informed them in advance of the notices in the carbarns, the union had attempted several times over the past month to meet with the company. The company had refused. Lowry would later say, like the union-buster that he was, that he preferred to deal with employees on an individual basis. The meeting in the temple wrapped up after a unanimous vote in favor of referring the dispute to a board of arbitration. Attendees who were not members of a committee that had been elected to meet with the company representatives were instructed to stay home and do nothing to disrupt the MSRC's functions.

In Bridge Square, ten thousand strikers and supporters gathered in protest. Someone suggested that they circulate petitions for government actions in both Minneapolis and St. Paul, where Lowry owned the St. Paul Street Railway Company. The suggestion met with resounding support. They would soon find out where the governments' loyalties lay.

That same morning, workers for the St. Paul Street Railway Company had found Lowry's notice in their carbarns. The men had gotten on their cable cars and kept the Saintly City running. That evening, they held a mass meeting, in the labor headquarters at 70 East Seventh Street in St. Paul. Strikers from the MSRC came to persuade them to strike as well, but the St. Paulite men didn't want to be too hasty. They referred the issue to the Knights of Labor District Executive Board.

Tensions were already boiling over in Minneapolis by the next morning, April 12. Charles Reynolds, an engineer with MSRC, was walking through the yard at the motor junction on his way to somewhere else when two of the appointed special policemen accosted him and made baseless accusations against him. They fought, and Reynolds got a cut on his head before Sergeant Kirkham of the Minneapolis Police Department came to his rescue. Reynolds, an innocent striker, was the first victim in the conflict between MSRC and its workers.

The streetcars still weren't running. More than one thousand men lounged around outside the MSRC HQ, rife with curiosity. What would happen next?

The Knights of Labor met with Lowry, who would concede nothing. That afternoon, three hundred men walked off the job in St. Paul, joining six hundred Minneapolitan men on strike. The Minneapolis strikers wouldn't have to worry about experienced, well-qualified strikebreakers from St. Paul taking their places on the MSRC cars.

Lowry was undaunted. He could always find inexperienced, unqualified strikebreakers. He and his brother-in-law and business associate, Calvin Gibson Goodrich, went with a police escort to the carbarn on Fourth Avenue South. It was only 1:00 p.m., and Lowry had already found strikebreakers. So far, he only had two of them: a driver and a conductor. They took a car from the barn as a crowd formed, roaring in protest. The rookie driver got the car stuck in the doorway on the way out of the barn, and he struggled with the horses, whom he couldn't manage well. It took him ten minutes to hit the road in earnest. A mob of strikers and sympathizers surrounded his car and stayed around it as it drove on. The driver didn't get far before someone unhitched his horses, sent them on their way and sent him on his way as well. Not long after that, the police boarded the car, and this time, the driver took it down to Fifth Street without interference. But there, at Fifth, the crowd surrounded the car and shouted at it. A man in the crowd handed the conductor a $10 bill, about $300 today. The conductor told the driver to take the car back to the barn. The crowd enjoyed that.

A second car went out at 2:30 p.m., with a police guard in an accompanying patrol wagon. It followed the route downtown and back again, but not without a spot of difficulty. Along Washington Avenue, a mob crowded the car, and the policemen had to force their way through. They soon took that car back out again. Straight out of the barn, a woman jumped aboard. Her name was Mrs. McCurdy. She and her husband, a college graduate, had lost all the money they had saved in a fire. He now worked as a streetcar driver, and they were barely scraping by.

"Won't you leave this car?" Mrs. McCurdy asked the strikebreaking driver. "[I]n taking this place you are taking bread out of the mouths of helpless women and children. Your mother would be ashamed to see you here...."

Leave this car and I will give you every dollar that I have, although I am a mother and my little child is at home now crying for bread. Will you not leave this car?[97]

The driver caved. He would leave, he said, if the conductor left too, but Mrs. McCurdy couldn't reach him in the same way. "I have got to make a living as well as you[,]" the conductor told her. "I'll give you fifty cents to quit this lecturing. If you don't stop you will have to get off."[98]

"I will pay my fare and ride as long as I choose," Mrs. McCurdy said. The conductor accepted her fare. As she realized that she wasn't making headway, she deboarded.

The car continued along Washington Avenue to the turntable. As it was heading back toward the barn, it passed a second car making its way down the line. The company had recruited more strikebreakers. The first car got to First Avenue South, when the mob boarded. They unhitched the horses and intimidated the driver and conductor back to the barn, without their car.

The second car had stopped on the turntable. The driver unhitched his horses and walked over to the first car to move it out of his way. Displaying incredible physical strength, he managed to make some progress with pushing it by hand. As he did so, a road tractor, hauling a trailer of wood, was crossing the street. Somebody in the crowd tugged out the kingpin that locked the trailer to the tractor. The load tumbled out onto the track. The second car on the turntable was trapped. The crowd grew, and the strikebreakers fled with the horses back to the barn, abandoning the cars. A sizable contingent of policemen failed to break up the mob. Late in the evening, the crowds still packed the streets. A patrol wagon full of policemen brought the cars home, and the company gave up strikebreaking for the day. Lowry had lost the battle, but he would win the war.

Earlier that afternoon, the executive committee of streetcar workers had published a proposition requesting arbitration with the company and agreeing to abide by the arbitrators' decision. The workers wanted the same thing as their fellow Minneapolitans, they said: "We have no wish to incommode our friends, the public, and are willing to take any steps consistent with honor and a due regard to our position, to start the cars to running on all lines in the city."[99] They suggested that accountants examine the finances of the MSRC. If Lowry really couldn't afford to pay them the rate agreed to in May 1888, then they would accept that. Lowry replied, "There will be no arbitration, none whatever. The notices posted mean exactly what they say. In future the Minneapolis railway will run its business to suit itself. No union shall be allowed to interfere in any way with our business."[100]

Minneapolitans walked home again that day, and still the strikers had their sympathy. In much-hillier St. Paul, reluctant pedestrians were more exasperated, but they resigned themselves to it after a generous bout of cursing. Every person with a rig—a horse hitched to a wheeled contrivance—made a tidy profit. They might have been the only citizens who were pleased with the situation. A threatening notice to striking workers in St. Paul was posted in the carbarns late on Friday night: any man who didn't return to work on Monday would be out of a job. Yet the strike wore on in both cities.

The petition that was dreamed up on the night of April 11 in Bridge Square had evolved. It called for the councils to ban special policemen, condemn strikebreaking and revoke the Lowry company street line licenses. Once the Northwestern Labor Union printed it, it garnered signatures from about twenty thousand registered voters within a matter of days. At that point, the petition was brought to the city councils with a demand that the alderman of each council request that the Minnesota state legislature allow the municipal governments to purchase the street railway franchise. On Tuesday, April 16, the St. Paul council voted in favor, but its request failed in the state legislature. The House passed a bill in support of permitting the city to purchase the franchise, but the Senate voted against it.

Lowry's companies started service again, with strikebreakers, and the riots started again too. Up until that point, the protesting had been nonviolent. Now the crowds, including women and children, derailed cars and strong-armed strikebreakers out of them. Once out of the cars, the strikebreakers were assaulted physically with battery and projectiles like stones, bricks and eggs. They were assaulted verbally as well. Rioters deliberately set paper cups, timber and torpedoes on the rails, and unhitched the horses. Off the streets, the strikebreakers couldn't duck inside for a quiet meal. Restaurateurs either refused to serve them food or failed to intervene when strikers and supporters harassed them while they ate. Before long, the strikebreakers were too demoralized to continue.

That was in Minneapolis. The riots never grew so vigorous in the capital, where supportive-but-staid St. Paulites simply declined to ride the streetcars. They continued to walk or to use a bus line that the strikers had organized. There wasn't much for the strikebreakers to do, and so they often deserted.

MSRC had to bring in strikebreakers from out of town. Some came from Chicago, but most were from Kansas City. Locals called them "cowboys" because they were always armed with revolvers, their drink of choice was whiskey and they chewed tobacco. The cowboys had among their number men who were experienced drivers and others who were professional strikebreakers. Regardless of their firearms, they couldn't show their faces in Minneapolis without being taunted or threatened.

Eva McDonald noticed a vicious cycle for the MSRC and its strikebreakers:

> *The new drivers and conductors, being persuaded to leave about as fast as the company hired them, those taking out the cars each day were unable to handle them skillfully. If a car ran off the track or a horse dropped dead from careless driving, the incident brought hundreds of people about in a few moments. At first the crowd would content themselves with calling "scab"* [a derogatory term for strikebreaker] *and ridiculing the new men. The obstruction of the first car soon blocked several others. The stopping of each car added to the excitement of the crowd. Missiles began to fly.*[101]

New workers would trip up, becoming vulnerable to rioters. The rioters would torment them to the utmost. Driven out of the city, they would be replaced by fresh faces, whose lack of experience would lead them into the same trap.

Fortunately, the police always appeared in time to interrupt the violence before anyone caused or received a significant injury. After the initial onslaught of a few patrolmen or mounted policemen breaking into the fray, the patrol wagon would swoop down on them with an extra load of policemen, who would make fifteen or twenty arrests and disperse the crowd for a time. Those arrested would receive the maximum penalties that the law permitted.

Sabotage abounded. It was a big enough deal when switches were stolen, but then turntables and stretches of track were taken as well.

A city councilor estimated that there were at least ten thousand unemployed men in Minneapolis, some of whom hadn't been able to find a job for several months despite being able-bodied and willing to work. "Yet out of this number," said McDonald, "not twenty could be hired at any price to take the places of the strikers."[102] People would rather go hungry than thwart the efforts of the strikers and face the community's wrath.

THE STRIKE WAS HARD on many Minneapolitans, as it was on workers who came from the suburbs. Before April 11, the streetcars had carried twenty-five thousand passengers per day. Makeshift buses and rigs couldn't make up the difference. Walking long miles into the city was tiring for those who lived far from the city center. Urban retailers took a hit. Shoppers had stopped making the trip downtown, not only because of the inconvenience of travel but also because of the rioting on the main thoroughfares along which the streetcars ran. Tourism had all but dried up. Still, 33 percent of Minneapolitans had signed the strikers' petition, and their rallies saw mass attendance.

Lowry's companies shelled out to pay the strikebreakers far more for their labor than he had his regular workers. More "cowboys" were brought in from the west, and yet fewer than half of the cars were running. The company requested, and got, police interference. Policemen were ordered to work on Lowry's cars as strikebreakers and to serve as hired muscle. If the strikers had needed any more evidence of government cooperation with MSRC, the city council of Minneapolis split its vote on the petition. It was April 19, Good Friday, eight days into the strike.

ON EASTER SUNDAY, INSTEAD of going to church, the men of the Riverside neighborhood stood around listlessly on the street. Holy day or not, they would have worked if there were any jobs available—not counting strikebreaking, that is. The Riverside streetcar line ran straight through their neighborhood, along Washington Avenue. The European immigrants who lived there resented the streetcars. *They* couldn't afford to ride them. The streetcars carried people with nice houses and steady jobs through *their* neighborhood on the way to and from work, filling it with the sound of clanging bells, forcing *their* children to interrupt their play to run out of the street to make way.

The Riverside men watched as well-dressed passengers rode by them on the streetcars. Eager to show up to church in their finery, there may have been people in those cars who supported the strike but made an exception for this one day. Policemen drove the cars, along with the cowboys, who prominently displayed their revolvers. There had been a report that the company had sent away the cowboys, but that had been false.

The Riverside men were too angry to be intimidated by officers of the law or firearms. They were ready for trouble. As far as they were concerned, the trouble was coming to them, and they were simply defending their home. Five thousand men had joined the throng on Washington Avenue by the end of the morning. The police ordered them back, and they obeyed. The crowd was growing by the hour. A few men threw stones at the cars, and the policemen phoned HQ to send backup.

Around 11:30 a.m., a southbound Riverside streetcar trundled along until it got to Eleventh Avenue South. The men in the crowd had stripped construction material from a nearby unfinished building and piled it onto the track. The driver didn't stop in time, and the car ran into the pile. The crowd hurled stones and bricks. The horses, driver and conductor bolted. The rioters shoved timbers under the car and cheered as it tipped over.

Another car approached from the north. The crowd surrounded it at Tenth Avenue South. A mounted police squad approached, but not quickly enough. The crowd threw stones at the car and shouted at the strikebreakers. They ran off, and so did some of the policemen. The mob tipped that car over too. They unhitched the horses, which bolted off to the barn. All hell broke loose:

> *The mounted and foot police drew their clubs and dashed into the crowd; for about a half an hour the people shrugged hither and thither regardless of police and refusing to disperse. The patrol wagons carried full loads to the police station. Some of those arrested being charged by the officers with tipping over the cars and disorderly conduct, but the great majority of the arrests were on the principle that if a man were among the crowd he was guilty and worthy of punishment.*[103]

Lowry "Himself Again."
Library of Congress: Chronicling America.

Twenty-odd men were arrested on the spot. The ones whom the police could not in good faith charge with offenses against persons or property were charged with the offense of "the gathering of more than three individuals on public streets."[104] The riot was contagious. All over the Mill City and all throughout the day, the main streets filled with agitated crowds. But do you know who *wasn't* among the mobs? Strikers. They didn't want any part of this. Their dispute with the MSRC had been the inspiration, but was not the substance, of the current unrest.

St. Paulites hadn't done anything like that at any point during the strike, but the company halted its cars in both cities that day.

It was all for nothing. Lowry got his way. The Minneapolis strikers saw that it didn't matter if the citizens had some common cause with them, because the company, the city council, the courts and law enforcement were in league against them. They didn't stand a chance. They voted to end the strike and go back to work, accepting their reduced pay. The company's lone concession was that the workers were no longer compelled to sign the "iron-clad" union-busting agreement.

MIDNIGHT ASSASSINATION

Thomas Flaherty, a stationary fireman, lived at 4606 Humboldt Avenue North in the Camden neighborhood. Around five o'clock in the afternoon on October 22, 1897, he was hard at work splitting wood in his yard.

"I'm shot!" said a man behind him. Flaherty looked up. He didn't recognize the man, whose face and clothes were bloody.

The stranger pointed to another man, who was walking down the street. "Here comes the man who shot and robbed me," said the stranger. "Catch him for God's sake. Catch him and pound him or I will pound him." He exclaimed, "Somebody follow him! Don't let him go!"[105]

William G. Beardsley, a market gardener, lived at 4609 Humboldt Avenue North. He was by his barn when he saw a tall, bloody, hatless man approaching. Beardsley overheard what the man said to Flaherty. The shooter, at that point, was less than one hundred feet away from them. Beardsley went to the injured man and helped him to walk to the porch of Flaherty's home and to lie down there. Someone called Dr. C.A. Smith. Mrs. Emma Poirier, who lived in the same house as Beardsley, tended to him for an hour. She helped Dr. Smith undress the victim so that he could see the wounds. Smith gave him a restorative and then had him brought to the city hospital.

While Mrs. Poirier and Smith helped the victim, Flaherty was keeping an eye on the shooter. He had barely altered his pace once the victim had identified him. He was walking toward the Minneapolis, St. Paul and Ste. Marie Railroad tracks, and Flaherty followed him. On the way, Flaherty stopped at a drugstore and used the phone to call the police. The shooter was walking so slowly that Flaherty caught up to him again, keeping a block's distance behind him. The man kept his right hand in his coat pocket, as if he were ready to draw and shoot. Flaherty followed him to a lumber yard. After a half-hour trip from his home, Flaherty abandoned his quest at Thirty-Sixth Avenue North and Washington. There, the man turned right, trudging on the gravel alongside the railroad tracks. Flaherty left off. This was a job for the police.

Earlier that day, Mrs. Anna Wenzel had given her younger brother John fifty cents and sent him out to find a job. He had only been staying with her and her family for a few days at their home in St. Paul. John was never home for long. He had spent his teenage years in and out of the St. Paul workhouse, the Ramsey County jail and the Iowa state prison. At nineteen, he was sent away to Stillwater prison for three years for highway robbery and was finally out. John was a compulsive thief, but he hadn't always been that way. Mrs. Wenzel remembered how normal and healthy he had been when he was little, back in Germany. Shortly after the family's arrival in America, when John was a preteen, he contracted a severe case of typhoid fever. He came out of a long stretch of delirium as a different child.

Their late mother had been mentally ill. She used to assault their father, long ago, before they had emigrated. She had once attacked him with a butcher's knife. She had suffered postpartum psychosis after the birth of one of her daughters and had tried to drown her. She was violent toward other family members and had even attacked Mrs. Wenzel's husband, Irvin. The children recognized that their mom was the problem, not them, and knew that she was ill.

After his fever, John gave her a run for her money. He started throwing prolonged tantrums, toddleresque in their intensity and irrationality, but laced with the profanity of a teenage boy. He would sometimes withdraw from the family, not speaking to anyone, encased in an invisible shell. He feared strangers. John never grew up—he grew down. He started taking things away from people—not to profit from it but because he wanted them for himself, just as a child would snatch away another child's toy to play with. Their mother, deranged but loving, devoted herself to helping John. Back then, in the days before the development of rehabilitative therapy, there wasn't much that parents could do for such a child. Their mother stretched herself thin, continuously bailing John out of trouble. Mrs. Wenzel believed that their mother's premature death had been caused by the strain of taking caring of John.

A decade later, John still preferred the company of children to that of adults and was enamored of marbles and spinning tops. Now that he was home, he played with the Wenzel children, which was nice, but he was *different*—even more different than he had been after the fever. He was constantly agitated, looking over his shoulder. He told Mr. and Mrs. Wenzel that "they" were coming for him. "They" were out to get him. "They" were sometimes stool pigeons who, he said, were watching his every move, and sometimes "they" were policemen, who would take him back to Stillwater.

He told Mrs. Wenzel that Stillwater liked repeat offenders because they already had experience with prison labor.

Before John left on his job search, Mrs. Wenzel asked him to shoot some rabbits that she saw as vermin and that her children treated as pets. The nervous, childlike young man refused and nearly wept as he told her that it would be cruel to kill their pets.

John Stavlo was born in Norway in March 1862 and was put to work on his parents' farm from a young age. He left school when he was twelve years old to become a seaman on his uncle's ship. After spending most of his teens in this manner, he returned home to work the land again. Well accustomed to manual labor, he came to Minneapolis at age eighteen, where he worked for lumber companies, in their lumber yards in the city and as a timberman in the woods. After that, he worked at railroad construction. He was thirty-four years old in 1886 when he joined Minneapolis PD.

John E. Morrisey had started out life on a farm too. He was twenty-three years old in 1881 when he moved to Minneapolis and started work as a streetcar driver. He joined Minneapolis PD five years later. In 1893, Morrisey and Stavlo were promoted to detective and proved that they deserved the position. They cracked high-profile cases in partnership with Hankinson and Hoy but also functioned at a high level when working primarily with each other. Now, they were put to the task of finding the shooter.

When Stavlo and Morrisey arrived on Humboldt Avenue North, Flaherty described the shooter's appearance to them and went with them into the woods west of Humboldt, south of Forty-Seventh Avenue North, covering the site of the present-day Humboldt Industrial Park. He thought that the shooter may have come from there. He was correct. Stavlo and Morrisey saw bloody leaves, and they plucked them from the trees for evidence.

Twenty-eight-year-old John Lemke had spent most of the past four years working as a machinist farther north, in Cloquet, Minnesota, but he had been living and working in Minneapolis for a few months. That day, on October 22, he had quit his job. He planned to visit his parents, who lived in Stillwater. He had $20 (about $654 today) in his pocket, and it must have been burning a hole. He went to Harry H. Green's jewelry and pawn broker shop at 213 Washington Avenue South. For $6 ($200 in modern currency), Lemke bought a lovely secondhand watch. It was a seventeen-jeweled Duber movement, in a Boss case. Green treated him to a glass of beer.

Lemke went to the Minneapolis Union Depot, which is now a site used for loading docks for the central downtown post office, located on the west bank of the Mississippi, south of Hennepin Avenue and north of Third Avenue South. The train provided passenger-only, intra-city transit. It may sound like a small operation, but the Stone Arch Bridge was built to accommodate it.

At the depot, a tall, handsome, well-built young man in a dark-gray coat and vest, dark-brown pants and a soft black hat struck up a conversation with Lemke. The man asked him about his work, including his wages, and Lemke answered his questions. The man asked him if he was new in Minneapolis or if he was familiar with it. Lemke replied that he knew it well enough. The man remarked that his new shoes were uncomfortable. He asked Lemke if he would go for a walk with him to break them in.

The man said that he had thirty cents for streetcar fare to Camden Place. They boarded the Camden Place streetcar at Hennepin and Washington Avenues around one o'clock in the afternoon. They rode to the end of the

The Mississippi River, as seen from the riverbank of North Minneapolis Regional Park, where Moshik shot Lemke. While they were sitting by the water, they may have had a view like this one. *Author's collection.*

Interpretive Center Greenery. This is the approximate area through which Lemke and Moshik walked on their way to the waterside. *Author's collection.*

line and then walked to the Minneapolis city workhouse at Fiftieth Avenue North and Lyndale. They walked past it and on to the riverbank, where they sat down. The man asked Lemke if he was interested in a criminal career. Lemke said that he was not. The man told him that he had only recently gotten out of Stillwater prison, where they had given him twenty-five dollars when he finished his sentence there, along with some clothes. He hadn't liked the clothes, and so he had ditched them and stolen someone else's from a clothesline.

The man asked Lemke if he would rob trains or commit burglary, and Lemke said that he wouldn't. The man reached into his pocket and took out a black false mustache. He announced that he was about to rob a farmer as he came walking up the road and that Lemke could hide behind a bush to "see how it was done."[106] The man put on his mustache. Lemke had no intention of witnessing a violent crime, so he jumped up, turned and ran. He made it about seven feet before the man shot him in the back with a .38-caliber revolver. Lemke fell, lying face-up. The man rolled him onto his stomach and shot him again. He beat Lemke over the head. He picked Lemke's pockets—taking his cash, pocket knife and his beautiful watch—and then he walked away, into the woods.

Shingle Creek, lined by a narrow thicket. Back then, there were more trees. Lemke left blood on the leaves as he staggered away from his killer. *Author's collection.*

Train Yard at Humboldt Industrial Park. This is the approximate location of the edge of the woods where Lemke emerged to find help. *Author's collection.*

This was the story that Lemke told Stavlo and Morrisey when they met him at the hospital. In the days before internet searches, centralized law enforcement databases or any form of official interagency cooperation, Stavlo and Morrisey had far fewer resources than the investigators of our era. Based solely on the information that Lemke and Flaherty had given them, the diligent duo managed to identify the assailant and learn his street address. Their suspect was John Moshik from St. Paul. Within a few hours of meeting Lemke at the hospital, Stavlo and Morrisey met with St. Paul Police authorities to ask for their help in making the arrest. The St. Paul police were at first reluctant to go along with it, as they were incredulous that Moshik had been the shooter. Eventually, the Minneapolis investigators persuaded them, and a few men from SPPD accompanied Stavlo and Morrisey to 1172 Reany Street.

Irwin Wenzel's brother-in-law had returned a little after six. He was quiet that evening and played with the children until they went to bed. After that, the men played cards together until late in the evening. They were getting ready to sleep when policemen knocked on the door.

John begged Wenzel not to let them in, but Wenzel moved toward the door. John took a watch from his pocket and pressed it into Wenzel's hand, telling him not to let the police know about it.

Mrs. Wenzel told the policemen that John had been home all day. She couldn't help but lie. John was practically in a fit, his eyes rolling. He backed up into a corner as the officers entered, and he shouted, "Keep away from me, you fellows! Keep away. Anna, don't let them take me!"[107] Mrs. Wenzel picked up a lamp and threw it at the police officers, missing them. After an energetic struggle, the policemen managed to strong-arm John outside. They called a patrol wagon, and as they were pushing him into it, he fought again, kicking one of the St. Paul policemen.

That was the end of the excitement on the case. Wenzel brought the watch to the police, who by then had searched the house and found the gun in the stove. They had also found Lemke's pocket knife on the ground after the struggle outside the Wenzel home. In Moshik's pocket, they found the black false mustache. Lemke died shortly around nine o'clock on Saturday, October 23. He had lived long enough to identify Moshik, whom the police brought to the hospital for that purpose. He did not live long enough, however, to see his devastated father, who had come to Minneapolis as soon as he heard the news about the shooting. Mr. Lemke missed his son by less than a day. John Lemke lost his life because he had shown consideration for, and trusted, a stranger.

MOSHIK'S ATTORNEY, T.A. GARRITY, a young man handling his first murder case, impressed everyone with his energetic defense of his client. Garrity argued that Moshik was not guilty by reason of insanity. He not only brought out Mrs. Wenzel to testify about his behavior since childhood, but he also called a witness to testify to a more recent occurrence. James McEvoy had served time at Stillwater prison and had witnessed one of the guards striking Moshik over the head with a three-quarter-inch-thick club, breaking the club into three pieces. Garrity also highlighted Moshik's strange demeanor in the wake of the shooting—how he had walked so casually down Humboldt even after Lemke had pointed him out to the residents. That, combined with the idiotic hiding place that he had chosen for the murder weapon, indicated to Garrity that Moshik was not in his right mind. The jury was not swayed by this extensive evidence of brain damage and mental illness. Moshik was found guilty and sentenced to death. And *that's* when things got crazy.

Minnesota papers had covered the murder, and the trial had attracted intense local interest. There were so many spectators that the judge had relocated to a larger courtroom to accommodate them. But interest in the case really exploded post-sentencing. Papers across the country, from Kansas and Indiana and Illinois and New York City clear down to Puerto Rico covered the Moshik saga. The story was printed in newspapers written in French, Spanish, Swedish, Polish and German. It's hard to say what, exactly, kicked it off. There were many factors at play. There was an ongoing investigation into abuses at Stillwater prison, and Moshik stated that he had once been sent to solitary confinement because a "stool pigeon" had lied to a guard and told him that Moshik had spoken at a time when the prisoners were supposed to be silent. Solitary, at Stillwater, didn't simply mean isolation. In the bare, solitary cell, the prisoner had to stick his arms through the bars at waist height, where the guard would handcuff him from outside the bars. The

John Moshik. *Library of Congress: Chronicling America.*

prisoner would stand like that all day, only being freed at night so that he could lie down to sleep.

After three days in solitary, Moshik was being escorted back toward his usual cell, but he didn't make it. On the way, he saw the man who had lied about him, and Moshik attacked him. As the guards were pulling him away, Moshik continued flailing and fighting. One of the guards struck Moshik over the head, and he was sent back to solitary. Moshik also said that he had been offered a deal to give false testimony against another man. Moshik explained the reason that he killed Lemke: he had thought that Lemke was one of the imaginary stool pigeons that, as he had previously told Mrs. Wenzel, were hunting him.

That would have been drama enough, of the most terrible kind, but Moshik also tried to escape from his cell at the Hennepin County Jail, located in what is now called the Municipal Building at 350 Fifth Avenue Street South. Most of the time, he exhibited signs of not knowing that he was going to be hanged. He was calm and cheerful and making plans for the future. Despite his severe difficulties, Moshik was brilliant. Everyone had always agreed with that, and the prosecutor had used the fact of his intelligence against him at trial, as evidence of his culpability. Years earlier, he had come up with the idea for a device that would use electricity to power vessels. He was still mulling over it now, in jail, and had hit on the idea of using a sort of millstone to generate the power. He said that he would make a lot of money off of it.

When he realized his position, Moshik tried to escape. On January 3, 1898, Special Watchman Peterson brought a pail of water and a mop to Moshik's cell so that he could clean his floor. This was something that Peterson did regularly. Things took a turn when Peterson opened the cell door. Moshik threw cigar ashes in his face, temporarily blinding him. Peterson grabbed him around the midsection, and Moshik hit him over the head with an iron hook that he had pulled off his bedstead. They grappled out of the cell, into the corridor. At the top of a stairway that led down to the cells below, Peterson finally lost his grip on the prisoner. Peterson couldn't see clearly, what with his own blood dripping into his eyes as well as the cigar ashes. Peterson had left his gun near Moshik's cell, and he shouted for Jailer Duffield before losing consciousness. Moshik snatched Peterson's keys and then left the cell, locking the watchman in the corridor. Moshik went out into the hallway. Street access could only be gained by the elevator. Moshik rang the elevator bell. The elevator operator recognized Moshik immediately and dropped down to the next floor so that Moshik could not try to force his

Minneapolis City Hall soon after completion. *Hennepin County Library Digital Collections.*

way inside. Duffield arrived with some deputy sheriffs, and they wrangled Moshik back into his cell.

Peterson's blood covered the floor and railings. He had sustained nine head wounds, one of which was three inches long and bone-deep. The wounds were non-fatal. Moshik said that they should all treat it as a joke.

Moshik also tried to escape by making an imitation gun out of paper and tinfoil and using it to intimidate Peterson. Peterson was not impressed.

Moshik bribed Peterson to bring him matches so that he could swallow them and attempt suicide that way. Peterson did so, but Moshik only vomited it all back up. The same went for the cigar stubs that he swallowed. He tried to bribe Peterson to help him escape, offering him $700 (about $23,000 today). It was the amount of Peterson's mortgage. Peterson agreed, but later Moshik said that he could only come up with $500. Peterson reneged and confessed the scheme to Hennepin County sheriff Alonzo Phillips, who fired him. Moshik's sister said that she had no idea how Moshik could possibly get $500, much less $700.

Like any celebrity, Moshik had his admirers. One woman brought him flowers and a book of quotes from the Bible.

Attorney Garrity filed a motion for a new trial, but it was denied. He eventually told Moshik's sisters, Mrs. Wenzel and a younger sister who had come from Montana, that he would continue to appeal without charging them for it. He would do it pro bono, but there would still be court fees that the sisters would have to cover. But he advised against further appeals, explaining that the effort had no chance of succeeding. Moshik was enraged at Garrity's advice and at his sisters' acceptance of it.

On January 25, Governor Clough signed Moshik's death warrant, fixing March 18 as the date of execution. Not long after that, a St. Paul dentist and hypnotist, Edward H. Haas, came out of the woodwork. He requested permission to hypnotize Moshik on the gallows. It would make for a fascinating scientific experiment, he said. Once Moshik was under hypnosis, Haas would tell Moshik that he was a grand person, very noble, very brave, and that his surroundings were peaceful and scenic. He would tell Moshik that he would feel no pain and that he should straighten all his muscles. Haas said that this might help him relax, betraying a confused perception of human physiology. He also said that this could prevent strangulation.

A physician in New York, who claimed to have attended many executions, argued that it was impossible for hypnosis to do any such thing. Minneapolitans hated Haas's idea because they didn't want a murderer to go to his doom while feeling on top of the world. The governor refused permission on the grounds that the entire point of a hanging was strangulation. The Haas sideshow was captured in papers all over the United States.

On April 24, 1889, Minnesota had debuted a statute that came to be known as the "midnight assassination law." Anti–death penalty state legislators, disgusted by the admission tickets to the Barrett brothers' hanging, had decided that executions should no longer be a source of entertainment for the masses. They must now be carried out during the dark, between midnight and five o'clock in the morning, and away from spectators. The only persons allowed to attend would be those who had some business there, such as the priest, sheriff, executioner and deputy sheriffs. This law was still in force nine years later, when it was Moshik's turn to hang.

The execution was to be carried out in a large, open area on the fifth floor. That area is now the waiting area for visitors at the Hennepin County Jail. At the time, it was bounded by the hospital wing and the "insane ward." The hanging was scheduled for 3:15 a.m., attended only by those people considered essential to the proceedings, including quite a few deputy sheriffs. Sheriff Phillips told the press that he planned to pull the lever on the trapdoor himself and that Moshik might break down emotionally.

ON THURSDAY, MARCH 18, at about half-past midnight, the deputy sheriffs began to arrive at the jail with their admission cards, which stated that the doors would open at one o'clock. There was only one elevator, with a maximum capacity of eight passengers. There were about one hundred men waiting for the elevator, and they brawled for it, afraid of missing the execution.

Moshik, his sisters and his priest, Father Jajelski, could hear the noise from his cell. Moshik thought that the crowd would tear him apart. Every time the elevator door opened, the four people in the cell heard the awful howls of the deputy sheriffs. Moshik begged Phillips to hang him that minute, preferring that to whatever the mob would do. Phillips refused.

There were 300 men on the jail floor by three o'clock. Moans of disappointment and anger came from the remaining 150 men still downstairs, who thought that they would miss the event. Phillips's regular deputies, not the mob of fools he had "deputized" for his own popularity and to win political favors, flung wide the doors to the open space, and they all rushed in, jockeying for a good view. They swigged their liquor while they waited.

Fifty feet away from the audience, Father Jajelski and Moshik were still in the cell, reciting the litany of the dying in spite of the noise from the throng. Duffield was engaged in crowd control, assuring the ticket-holders that everyone would be allowed in. The "deputies" cheered. By 3:15 a.m., they were settled down and admiring a cat that had snuck in. It jumped down on the trap of the gallows. It was enticed off it and was swept up by a man in the audience. At 3:20 a.m., Duffield spoke again, asking them to be patient while they waited for some more of Phillips's friends who were still downstairs. It was only fair, said Duffield, that they hold off on the execution until those remaining men arrived. Duffield insisted that it would only take ten more minutes and that it would be worth the wait. Some men applauded this, and others hissed.

Everyone and everything was in place at half-past three, and the crowd settled down for the show. Moshik came to the door and paused there, saying goodbye to his sisters for the last time. He had wanted them to be there until the end, but Jajelski and Phillips had persuaded him to let them go. Moshik stepped out into the open space, the site of his execution, wearing a black shroud and a cap. He seemed to barely notice the crowd as he stepped onto the trap. When asked if he had any last words, he said that he did not. He instructed his executioners to tug his bounds tighter. They obliged and then pulled the cap over his face. Jajelski stepped aside, and Phillips pulled the lever. The cap slipped off Moshik's head, revealing his distorted face. The crowd suddenly became unsettled.

Jajelski went to sob in a corner. Phillips was shaken, and he went to Jajelski for comfort. Ten minutes later, a doctor pronounced Moshik dead. Duffield thanked the crowd for their courtesy, and that was the end of the show.

At 9:00 a.m., Jajelski said the requiem Mass for the dead at the Polish Catholic Church at Fourth Street and Seventeenth Avenue Northeast in Minneapolis. The service was well attended, thanks to the morbidly curious, but the crowd faded away once the family took the remains for interment. John Moshik, a damaged, violent man who never had a chance at life, lies buried at St. Mary's Cemetery, at 4403 Chicago Avenue South.

NOTES

Part I

1. Soldiers at the fort witnessed this event. Along with every other story covered in this section, the account is filtered through a Euro-American cultural lens.
2. White historians documented a Dakota story that the Ojibwe-Dakota rivalry began with an elaborate fight over a girl. We have to be careful about accepting non-Native recountings of such tales because of possible mistranslations and misunderstandings. In addition, a group of Natives confessed to a visiting Italian statesman that "when they go down to the raiders' settlements, they amuse themselves with gulling their credulity by a number of fables, which afterwards become the oracles of geographers and book-makers." *Beltrami Journal*, quoting Neill, *History of Minnesota*, 371. Basically, there were *some* Natives who were messing with whites for fun, and now it's difficult to sort out what was genuine legend and what was intentional nonsense.
3. Man of the Sky was more commonly called "Cloud Man" by Euro-Americans, but he signed his own name as "Man of the Sky." He also estimated his year of birth as 1795. However, multiple reliable accounts from that time indicate that he was born an entire decade earlier.
4. "Chief" corresponds approximately to "mayor" or "governor." I have kept the term "chief" here for the sake of simplicity. This does not imply that it is the only English-language term for this leadership role.
5. Numerous Native nations were involved as well, but that's not pertinent to this story.
6. Folwell, *Minnesota*, 62.
7. Snelling, "Running the Gantlet," 440.
8. Folwell, *Minnesota*, 62.
9. Here, he meant the Sacs and Fox, who also raided the Dakotas.
10. Gary C. Anderson, "The Removal of the Mdewakanton Dakota in 1837: A Case for Jacksonian Paternalism," *South Dakota History* 10 (Fall 1980), 328n, quoted in Dietrich, "'Good Man' in a Changing World," 15.

11. There were two men, father and son, named Hole in the Day: Hole in the Day (the Elder) and Hole in the Day (the Younger), comparable to "Senior/Sr." and "Junior/Jr." In this chapter, and the ones that follow, "Hole in the Day" refers to the Elder, and his son will be referred to specifically as "Hole in the Day (the Younger)." Another important note about Hole in the Day (the Elder) is that although he comes across as the antagonist in this section of the book, that is because these accounts come from the allies and sympathizers of the Dakotas. Hole in the Day was fighting for his people when he expanded their hunting grounds at the Dakotas' expense.

12. Taliaferro, *Taliaferro Journals*, vol. 15, Journal, August 2, 1838.

13. The two groups had a close alliance with the Potawatomis as well, but the full trifecta is not germane here.

14. Taliaferro took notes at all of these councils. For this reason, we have precise accounts of not only this meeting but also the ones that follow.

15. "(war)" is either Taliaferro's parenthetical note for clarification, or his representation of The Good Road's delivery. It's not clear in Taliaferro's notes.

16. Taliaferro, *Taliaferro Journals*, August 4, 1838.

17. Ibid., August 8, 1838.

18. Stevens, *Minnesota and Its People*, 398–99.

19. Henry H. Sibley in the *Pioneer Press*, May 13, 1894, found in Folwell, *History of Minnesota*, 1:157.

20. Dietrich, "'Good Man' in a Changing World," 16.

21. Deanne Z. Weber, "Childhood Among the Dakota, Jane Gibbs: 'Little Bird that Was Caught,'" *Ramsey County History* 31 (Spring 1996): 8, quoted in Dietrich, "'Good Man' in a Changing World," 16. They sang other songs as well. Jane Gibbs, a white child living at Bde Maka Ska, learned that song in particular.

22. This is yet another story with multiple versions because of the disputed narrative even at the time.

23. Folwell, *History of Minnesota*, 1:196.

24. Stevens, *Minnesota and Its People*, 3.

25. There is dispute between sources regarding the timing of events in this chapter but not the events themselves. It all occurred between the 1840s and mid-1850s, however.

26. Atwater, *History of the City of Minneapolis*, 81.

27. Ibid., 80.

28. Ibid., 81.

Part II

29. In keeping with the extreme fickleness of a Minneapolis June, the temperature soared to ninety-five degrees Fahrenheit by June 23, according to "ANNUAL CLIMATOLOGICAL SUMMARY."

30. Stevens, *Minnesota and Its People*, 287 (original spelling and punctuation retained).

31. Ibid.
32. Mead and Muller, *History of the Police and Fire Departments*, 33; Grey and Harpole, "Black Community in Territorial St. Anthony," 52.
33. Best Places, "Minneapolis, Minnesota."
34. CBS Minnesota, "Forbes Votes Minneapolis 6th Most Liberal City."
35. Key Land Homes, "*US News* Ranks Minneapolis & St. Paul Among Most Diverse Cities."
36. Folwell, *Minnesota*, 149.
37. Ibid.
38. Grey and Harpole, "Black Community in Territorial St. Anthony," 51.
39. They also cited the fact of their legal marriage—a right that was reserved for free persons, as Taliaferro would have known.
40. This is the correct spelling of the defendant's name. "Sandford" was a typo in the court record.
41. Mead and Muller, *History of the* Police *and Fire Departments*, 33.
42. Ibid.
43. Ibid., 70.
44. Folwell, *History of Minnesota*, 2:69.
45. "Minneapolis 'Slave' Case."

Part III

46. Folwell, *History of Minnesota*, 3:57.
47. The phrase "Dark Satanic Mills" comes from William Blake's 1808 poem "Jerusalem."
48. Anfinson, "Fickle Partner," 109.
49. Ibid., 108.
50. "Jubilate!"
51. Kane, *Falls of St. Anthony*, 69.
52. Welles, *Autobiography and Reminiscences*, 2:165.
53. Ibid., 166.
54. Ehrman-Solberg, "Minneapolis Is Ruined."
55. Welles, *Autobiography and Reminiscences*, 2:168.
56. *St. Paul Daily Press*, October 6, 1869, quoted in Kane, *Falls of St. Anthony*, 71–72.
57. Welles, *Autobiography and Reminiscences*, 2:169.
58. Ibid., 170.
59. "The Situation."
60. *New York Graphic*, May 10, 1878, quoted in Kane, *Falls of St. Anthony*, 102–3.
61. Ibid.
62. Folwell, *History of Minnesota*, 3:134.
63. Costello, *History of the Fire and Police Departments of Minneapolis*, 62.
64. Ibid., 61.
65. Quoted in Atwater and Stevens, *Minneapolis and Hennepin County*, 624.

Part IV

66. Costello, *History of the Fire and Police Departments of Minneapolis*, 243.
67. Stevens, *Minnesota and Its People*, 287.
68. Northern Illinois University Digital Library, "Minneapolis Tragedy," 5.
69. Ibid., 7.
70. Ibid., 15.
71. Ibid., 7.
72. Ibid., 8.
73. Ibid., 10.
74. Ibid., 11.
75. Ibid.
76. Ibid., 14.
77. Ibid., 16.
78. Ibid.
79. Ibid., 15.
80. Ibid.
81. Ibid., 14.
82. "Barrett Trial," 3.
83. "Brothers on the Scaffold."
84. "Brothers Will Hang."
85. "Not Yet Ready," 3.
86. "Who Did the Deed?," 5.
87. "Fight for Life," 3.
88. "He Flies High," 3.
89. "Brothers on the Scaffold."
90. Gay, *Tale of the Twin Cities*, 5. Most of the quotations in this chapter come from Gay's book. In all of them, the original spelling is retained.
91. Quoted in Gay, *Tale of the Twin Cities*, 7–8.
92. Quoted in Gay, *Tale of the Twin Cities*, 9.
93. Quoted in Gay, *Tale of the Twin Cities*, 8.
94. Gay, *Tale of the Twin Cities*, 10.
95. Ibid., 12.
96. Ibid.
97. Ibid., 17.
98. Ibid., 18.
99. Ibid., 19.
100. Ibid., 20.
101. Ibid., 54–55.
102. Ibid., 55.
103. Ibid., 64.
104. Faue, *Writing the Wrongs*, 61.
105. "Story of the Fate of John Lemke," 4.
106. "Justice Is Active," 2.
107. "Doesn't Deny His Crime," 3.

BIBLIOGRAPHY

African American Registry. "Eliza Winston, Domestic Worker Born." https://
aaregistry.org/story/eliza-winston-born.

Anfinson, John O. "A Fickle Partner: Minneapolis and the Mississippi River." In
The City, the River, the Bridge: Before and After the Minneapolis Bridge Collapse. Edited by
Patrick Nunnally. Minneapolis: University of Minnesota Press. 2011.

"Annual Climatological Summary. Ft. Snelling MN. Year 1856." Department
of Natural Resources, Minnesota's State Portal. https://files.dnr.state.mn.us/
natural_resources/climate/twin_cities/1856sum.html.

Atwater, Isaac. *History of the City of Minneapolis, Minnesota*. New York: Munsell &
Company, Publishers, 1893.

Atwater, Isaac, and John H. Stevens. *Minneapolis and Hennepin County, Minnesota*. Vol.
1. New York: Munsell Publishing Company, 1895.

"The Barrett Trial. The Counsel for the Defense Got in Some Shoulder Blows
Yesterday. Evidence of the Cyclone Detective of the Northwest Remains
Unshaken. 'Reddy' Barrett Fails to Identify the Pistol Chamberlain Found.
The Prosecution Has a Little Scheme to Jog the Memory of Tim." *St. Paul
Daily Globe*, December 31, 1887. Chronicling America: Historic American
Newspapers, Library of Congress. https://chroniclingamerica.loc.gov/lccn/
sn90059522/1887-12-31/ed-1/seq-3.

"Became a Turbulent Mob. People Who Had Cards to Moshik's Execution.
How the John Day Smith Law that Aimed at Secret and Mysterious Executions
Was Observed in His Own Town—Jests and Small Bottles Were the Other
Features of the Hanging." *St. Paul Globe*, March 19, 1898. Chronicling
America: Historic American Newspapers, Library of Congress. https://
chroniclingamerica.loc.gov/lccn/sn90059523/1898-03-19/ed-1/seq-6.

Bergen, Peter. "Al-Shabaab's American Allies." *CNN Opinion*, September 24, 2013. https://www.cnn.com/2013/09/23/opinion/bergen-al-shabaab-americanties/index.html.

Bessler, John D. *Legacy of Violence: Lynch Mobs and Executions in Minnesota*. Minneapolis: University of Minnesota Press, 2003.

Best Places. "Minneapolis, Minnesota. Politics & Voting in Minneapolis, Minnesota." https://www.bestplaces.net/voting/city/minnesota/minneapolis.

"Brothers on the Scaffold. They Were Together in Crime and in Death Not Divided. The Barrett Boys Swung Off. History of a Crime Which Blackens a Family Name and Creates Bitter Enmity Among Survivors." *Omaha Daily Bee*, March 23, 1889. Chronicling America: Historic American Newspapers, Library of Congress. https://chroniclingamerica.loc.gov/lccn/sn99021999/1889-03-23/ed-1/seq-1.

"Brothers Will Hang. After Repeated Delays the Supreme Court Refuses the Barretts' Appeal. Killed a Car Driver for the Contents of His Cash Box. Bravado and Bluff Greet the Jailer Who Conveys the Bad News. A Death Watch Set Upon the Movements of the Condemned." *St. Paul Daily Globe*, January 29, 1889. Chronicling America: Historic American Newspapers, Library of Congress. https://chroniclingamerica.loc.gov/lccn/sn90059522/1889-01-29/ed-1/seq-1.

Brueggemann, Gary. *Minnesota's Oldest Murder Mystery: The Case of Edward Phalen, St. Paul's Unsaintly Pioneer*. Eden Prairie, MN: Beaver's Pond Press, 2013.

"By the Hypnotic Route." *Willmar Tribune*, February 15, 1898. Chronicling America: Historic American Newspapers, Library of Congress. https://chroniclingamerica.loc.gov/lccn/sn89081022/1898-02-15/ed-1/seq-7.

CBS Minnesota. "Forbes Votes Minneapolis 6th Most Liberal City." https://minnesota.cbslocal.com/2015/07/16/forbes-votes-minneapolis-6th-most-liberal-city.

"Chain Is Complete. Witnesses Tell in Court the Story of John Moshik's Crime. Not a Shadow of Doubt. Defense Will Rely on a Plea of Insanity to Secure Light Sentence." *St. Paul Globe*, December 3, 1897. Chronicling America: Historic American Newspapers, Library of Congress. https://chroniclingamerica.loc.gov/lccn/sn90059523/1897-12-03/ed-1/seq-3.

Costello, Augustine E. *History of the Fire and Police Departments of Minneapolis: Their Origin, Progress and Development*. Minneapolis, MN: Relief Publishing Company, 1890.

"The Courts and Bar of Hennepin County." *Illustrated Minneapolis: A Souvenir of the Minneapolis Journal*. 1891. The Minnesota Legal History Project, July 1, 2021. http://www.minnesotalegalhistoryproject.org/assets/Cts%20&%20Bar%20of%20Henn.%20Cty%20(1891).pdf.

Dietrich, Mark. "A 'Good Man' in a Changing World: Man of the Sky, the Dakota Leader, and His Life and Times." *Ramsey County History* 36, no. 1 (Spring 2001): 4–24.

"Doesn't Deny His Crime. Plea of Insanity Is the Defense in Moshik Trial." *St. Paul Globe*, December 4, 1897. Chronicling America: Historic American Newspapers, Library of Congress. https://chroniclingamerica.loc.gov/lccn/sn90059523/1897-12-04/ed-1/seq-3.

Ehrman-Solberg, Kevin. "'Minneapolis Is Ruined': The Tunnel Disaster of 1869." *Historyapolis*, February 22, 2016. http://historyapolis.com/blog/2016/02/22/minneapolis-is-ruined-the-tunnel-disaster-of-1869.

"Excitement in Minneapolis." *Weekly Pioneer and Democrat*, August 24, 1860. Chronicling America: Historic American Newspapers, Library of Congress. https://chroniclingamerica.loc.gov/lccn/sn83016751/1860-08-24/ed-1/seq-6

Faue, Elizabeth. *Writing the Wrongs: Eva Valesh and the Rise of Labor Journalism*. Ithaca, NY: Cornell University Press, 2002.

"A Fiend Lynched." *St. Charles Union*, May 3, 1882. Minnesota Digital Newspaper Hub, Minnesota Historical Society. https://newspapers.mnhs.org/jsp/PsImageViewer.jsp?doc_id=4394ddb9-ec76-44fa-bc60-1a7beca0b761%2Fmnhi0031%2F1HMBCO58%2F82050301.

"A Fight for Life. The Trial of Barrett Drags Its Weary Length Along at Minneapolis." *St. Paul Daily Globe*, February 7, 1888. Chronicling America: Historic American Newspapers, Library of Congress. https://chroniclingamerica.loc.gov/lccn/sn90059522/1888-02-07/ed-1/seq-3.

Find a Grave. "John Whittemore Eastman." December 15, 2011. https://www.findagrave.com/memorial/81988144/john-whittemore-eastman.

———. "Lilla F Spear." December 27, 2013. https://www.findagrave.com/memorial/122301863/lilla-f-spear.

———. "Mina Luette Spear Childs." December 20, 2015. https://www.findagrave.com/memorial/156217147/mina-luette-childs.

———. "William Wallace Eastman." January 7, 2010. https://www.findagrave.com/memorial/46428391/william-wallace-eastman.

Folwell, William Watts. *A History of Minnesota*. Vol. 1. St. Paul: Minnesota Historical Society, 1922.

———. *A History of Minnesota*. Vol. 2. St. Paul: Minnesota Historical Society, 1924.

———. *A History of Minnesota*. Vol. 3. St. Paul: Minnesota Historical Society, 1926.

———. *Minnesota: The North Star State*. Boston: Houghton Mifflin, 1908.

Gates, Charles M., and H. "The Tourist Traffic of Pioneer Minnesota." *Minnesota History* 16, no. 3 (1935): 272–81.

Gay, Eva. *A Tale of the Twin Cities: Lights and Shadows of the Street Car Strike in Minneapolis and St. Paul, Minnesota, Beginning April 11, 1889*. Minneapolis, MN: From the Press of Thos. A. Clark & Company, 1889.

Grey, Emily O. Goodridge, and Patricia C. Harpole. "The Black Community in Territorial St. Anthony: A Memoir." *Minnesota History* 49, no. 2 (Summer 1984): 42–53.

Hansen, Marcus L. *Old Fort Snelling, 1819–1858*. Iowa City: State Historical Society of Iowa, 1918.

"He Flies High, Does County Attorney Davis in His Address. Detectives Are Defended. Hints for Wealthy Citizens About to Die—Argument in the Murder Case." *St. Paul Daily Globe*, February 17, 1888. Chronicling America: Historic American Newspapers, Library of Congress. https://chroniclingamerica.loc.gov/lccn/sn90059522/1888-02-17/ed-1/seq-3.

"The Hennepin County Slave Case—Triumph of the 'Freedom Shriekers.'" *Weekly Pioneer and Democrat*, August 24, 1860. Chronicling America: Historic American Newspapers, Library of Congress. https://chroniclingamerica.loc.gov/lccn/sn83016751/1860-08-24/ed-1/seq-6.

Historic Fort Snelling, Minnesota Historical Society. "The Ojibwe People." https://www.mnhs.org/fortsnelling/learn/native-americans/ojibwe-people.

Huber, Molly. "Lowry, Thomas (1843–1909)." *MNopedia*, April 14, 2015. Minnesota Historical Society. http://www.mnopedia.org/person/lowry-thomas-1843-1909.

Hudson, Horace B. "Courts and Lawyers of Minneapolis." *A Half Century of Minneapolis*. 1908. The Minnesota Legal History Project. http://www.minnesotalegalhistoryproject.org/assets/Courts%20and%20Lawyers%20of%20Mpls%20(1908)=VVV.pdf.

"Hypnotized, Then Hanged." *Wichita Daily Eagle*, February 20, 1898. Chronicling America: Historic American Newspapers, Library of Congress. https://chroniclingamerica.loc.gov/lccn/sn82014635/1898-02-20/ed-1/seq-10.

"Jubilate!" *Minneapolis Daily Tribune*, March 17, 1869. Minnesota Digital Newspaper Hub, Minnesota Historical Society. https://newspapers.mnhs.org/jsp/PsImageViewer.jsp?doc_id=e5cc789a-0864-47b2-887e-008c5eeb70dc%2Fmnhi0005%2F1DFC5656%2F69031701.

"Justice Is Active. Web of Evidence Being Woven Around John Moshik. Jury Charges Murder. Incidents of Yesterday Connected with Lemke's Death." *Minneapolis Tribune*, October 26, 1897. Minnesota Digital Newspaper Hub, Minnesota Historical Society. https://newspapers.mnhs.org/jsp/PsImageViewer.jsp?doc_id=4a0c6900-28ec-40e6-bafa-8705a70f68f8%2Fmnhi0005%2F1DFC5F59%2F97102601.

Kane, Lucille M. *The Falls of St. Anthony: The Waterfall that Built Minneapolis*. St. Paul: Minnesota Historical Society Press, 1987.

Kelsey, Kerck. *Remarkable Americans: The Washburn Family*. Gardiner, ME: Tilbury House Publishers, 2008.

Key Land Homes. "*US News* Ranks Minneapolis & St. Paul Among Most Diverse Cities." https://keylandhomes.com/us-news-ranks-minneapolis-st-paul-among-most-diverse-cities.

"Like a Besom. The Terrible Explosion Last Evening Which Carried with It Death and Destruction. The Most Direful Calamity Which Has Ever Befallen the City of Minneapolis. Five Flouring Mills and Other Valuable Buildings Scattered in Countless Fragments. Relentless Flames Finish the Work of Devastation with Horrible Completeness. Sixteen Persons Known to Be Killed—The Bodies of the Poor Victims Consumed. Terrible Force of the Explosion—The Intense Excitement throughout the City. The Spectacle Last Night During the Progress of the Conflagration—Painful Scenes. Wild Despair of the Wives, Parents, and Children of the Poor Victims. The Fuller Realization of the Extent of the Calamity This Morning. Evidences of the Tremendous Force of the Explosion Found in All Parts of the City. Interviews with Daniel A. Day and Alexander Bradley, Two of the Wounded. Estimate of the Losses—Nearly Complete List of the Insurance. The Force of the Shock at St. Paul—Excitement and Consternation in That City. Complete List of the Dead and Wounded—Narrow Escapes—Miscellaneous Notes." *Minneapolis Tribune*, May 3, 1878. Minnesota Digital Newspaper Hub, Minnesota Historical Society. https://newspapers.mnhs.org/jsp/PsImageViewer.jsp?doc_id=7fe71607-29e4-48e3-947a-9665b6f6fc5c%2Fmnh i0005%2F1DFC5C57%2F78050301.

Marcy-Holmes Neighborhood Association. "Winslow House Hotel (1856)." Minneapolis Historical. https://minneapolishistorical.org/items/show/99.

Mead, Frank J., and Alix J. Muller. *History of the Police and Fire Departments of the Twin Cities: Their Origin in Early Village Days and Progress to 1900. Historical and Biographical*. Minneapolis, MN: American Land & Title Register Association, 1899.

"The Minneapolis 'Slave' Case." *St. Cloud Democrat*, September 6, 1860. Chronicling America: Historic American Newspapers, Library of Congress. https://chroniclingamerica.loc.gov/lccn/sn83016836/1860-09-06/ed-1/seq-1.

Neill, Edward D. *The History of Minnesota: From the Earliest Explorations to the Present Time*. Philadelphia, PA: J.B. Lippincott & Company, 1858.

Neill, Edward D., and Fletcher Williams. *History of Hennepin County and the City of Minneapolis, Including the Explorers and Pioneers of Minnesota by Rev. Edward D. Neill, and Outlines of the History of Minnesota, by Fletcher Williams*. Minneapolis, MN: North Star Publishing Company, 1881.

Northern Illinois University Digital Library. "'The Minneapolis Tragedy: Full Account of the Crime of the Fiend Frank McManus, and the Swift Retribution of an Outraged Community.' Mark Twain's Mississippi." 1882. https://digital.lib.niu.edu/islandora/object/niu-twain%3A10903.

"NOT YET READY. The State Asks for Time in the Car-Driver Murder Case. THE BARRETTS IN COURT. Comment on Their Youthful Appearance—Scenes Before the Examination in the Municipal Court." *St. Paul Daily Globe*, November 29, 1887. Chronicling America: Historic American Newspapers, Library of Congress. https://chroniclingamerica.loc.gov/lccn/sn90059522/1887-11-29/ed-1/seq-3.

Pennefeather, Shannon M. *Mill City: A Visual History of the Minneapolis Mill District*. St. Paul: Minnesota Historical Society, 2003.

Porter, Beverly J. *The Hub of Hell: A True Story of a Nineteenth-Century Neighborhood, Murder, and Trial*. Grand Rapids, MI: Credo House Publishers, 2019.

Schenck, Theresa M. *William W. Warren: The Life, Letters, and Times of an Ojibwe Leader*. Lincoln: University of Nebraska Press, 2007.

"A Shocking Outrage. The Little Daughter of Mr. and Mrs. Jason Spear Outraged by a Tramp. The Deed Done in Broad Daylight—The Victim's Condition—The Terrible Particulars. Captured and Placed in Custody—The Fiend Confesses His Guilt—An Indignant Community. LATER—Indignant Crowds Rally and March on the County Jail. In Complete Possession at 2:30 This Morning—The Corridors Full of Masked Men. Blows of Sledge Hammers Resounding—Breaking in the Iron Doors of the Cells." *Minneapolis Tribune*, April 28, 1882. Minnesota Digital Newspaper Hub, Minnesota Historical Society. https://newspapers.mnhs.org/jsp/PsImageViewer.jsp?doc_id=7fe71607-29e4-48e3-947a-9665b6f6fc5c%2Fmnhi0005%2F1DFC5C58%2F82042801.

"The Situation." *Minneapolis Daily Tribune*, October 8, 1869. Minnesota Digital Newspaper Hub, Minnesota Historical Society. https://newspapers.mnhs.org/jsp/PsImageViewer.jsp?doc_id=e5cc789a-0864-47b2-887e-008c5eeb70dc%2Fmnhi0005%2F1DFC5656%2F69100801.

Snelling, William Joseph. "Running the Gantlet: A Thrilling Incident of Early Days at Fort Snelling." *Annals of the Society*. 1856. Reprint, St. Paul: Minnesota Historical Society, 1872.

Steffens, Lincoln. *The Shame of the Cities*. New York: McClure, Phillips, and Company, 1904.

Stevens, John H. *Minnesota and Its People, and Early History of Minneapolis*. Minneapolis, MN: Tribune Job Printing Company, 1890.

"STORY OF THE FATE OF JOHN LEMKE TOLD IN COURT. Complete Chain of Evidence Woven Around John Moshik, On Trial Charged with a Cruel Murder—Every Witness Who Testified Yesterday Added to the Weight of the Accusation Against the Prisoner—Every Detail, from the Finding of the Victim in the Woods, Down to the Time of His Death, and the Arrest of Moshik, Graphically Depicted. *Minneapolis Tribune*, December 3, 1897. Minnesota Digital Newspaper Hub, Minnesota Historical Society. https://newspapers.mnhs.org/jsp/PsImageViewer.jsp?doc_id=4a0c6900-28ec-40e6-bafa-8705a70f68f8%2Fmnhi0005%2F1DFC5F59%2F97120301.

Taliaferro, Lawrence. *Taliaferro Journals*. Vol. 15. Transcript. Journal, May–November 1838; April–June 1839. Location P1203, Box 7. Lawrence Taliaferro Papers, Minnesota Historical Society, St. Paul, Minnesota.

"A Terrible Crime Justly Avenged." *New Ulm Review*, May 3, 1882. Minnesota Digital Newspaper Hub, Minnesota Historical Society. https://newspapers.mnhs.org/jsp/PsImageViewer.jsp?doc_id=03d10257-263d-416b-9573-60a6ef43ae3a%2Fmnhi0031%2F1H0YY358%2F82050301.

Trenerry, Walter N. *Murder in Minnesota: A Collection of True Cases*. St. Paul: Minnesota Historical Society, 1962. Reprint, 1985.

Van Cleve, Charlotte Ouisconsin. *"Three Score Years and Ten": Lifelong Memories of Fort Snelling, Minnesota, and Other Parts of the West*. Minneapolis: Printing House Harrison & Smith, 1888.

Welles, Henry Titus. *Autobiography and Reminiscences.* Vol. 2. Minneapolis, MN: Printed by M. Robinson, 1899.

"WHO DID THE DEED? The State Rests in the Tollefson Case and the Defense Begins. It Charges 'Reddy' Barrett with Having Murdered the Driver. Tim Barrett Takes the Stand and Proves a Poor Witness. Interest at Its Height and the Case Absorbing Much Attention." *St. Paul Daily Globe*, December 27, 1887. Chronicling America: Historic American Newspapers, Library of Congress. https://chroniclingamerica.loc.gov/lccn/sn90059522/1887-12-27/ed-1/seq-6.

Why Treaties Matter. "Multinational Treaties at Prairie Du Chien." http://treatiesmatter.org/treaties/land/1825-1830-Multinational.

Woods, Donald Z. "Playhouse for Pioneers: The Story of the Pence Opera House." *Minnesota History* 33, no. 4. (Winter 1952): 169–78.

Wyman, James T. "Manufactures." In *History of Minneapolis and Hennepin County.* Vol. 1. Edited by Isaac Atwater and John H. Stevens. New York: Munsell Publishing Company, 1895, 526–690.

Young, Biloine Whiting. *River of Conflict, River of Dreams: Three Hundred Years on the Upper Mississippi.* Canada: Pogo Press, 2004.

INDEX

ABOUT THE AUTHOR

Ron de Beaulieu has lived in South Minneapolis for about six years, and no amount of snow has kept her from walking along Minnehaha Creek almost every day. Before that, when she lived in Southeast, no amount of snow kept her from walking along the Mississippi River almost every day (wind chill was a different story). Exploring the Mill City never gets old for Ron. She has earned graduate degrees in history and sociology, with a focus on criminology, and considers herself lucky to have had the opportunity to combine her research interests with her hobby.